Chaplaincy Ministry and the
Mission of the Church

Chaplaincy Ministry and the Mission of the Church

Victoria Slater

scm press

© Victoria Slater 2015

Published in 2015 by SCM Press
Editorial office
3rd Floor
Invicta House
108–114 Golden Lane
London, EC1Y 0TG

SCM Press is an imprint of Hymns Ancient & Modern Ltd
(a registered charity)
13A Hellesdon Park Road
Norwich NR6 5DR, UK

www.scmpress.co.uk

British Library Cataloguing in Publication data

A catalogue record for this book is available
from the British Library

978 0 334 05315 6

Typeset by Manila Typesetting Company

Printed and bound by CPI Group (UK) Ltd.

Contents

Acknowledgements

This book could not have been written without the generosity of a wide community of people who have been willing to share with me their experience of and insights into chaplaincy ministry. I would like to thank the Oxford Centre for Ecclesiology and Practical Theology (OxCEPT) at Ripon College Cuddesdon for supporting the initial research upon which this book is based. Special thanks are due to everyone who shared with me their experience of chaplaincy ministry as participants in the research. Your reflections and insights have helped me to shape my thinking about chaplaincy ministry and, in return, I hope that this book may contribute to your own thinking about and development of chaplaincy.

My initial hunch about the contemporary significance of chaplaincy ministry would not have been developed without the support and encouragement of Helen Cameron, Zoe Bennett, David Lyall, Vernon Trafford and my peers who were part of the learning community on the Professional Doctorate in Practical Theology at Anglia Ruskin University. In particular, I would like to thank Helen Cameron who has provided practical wisdom and unfailing support throughout my engagement with this subject. Thanks are also due to Margaret Whipp and Guy Harrison for their comments and encouragement.

It has been a privilege to explore chaplaincy ministry with so many people over the past five years and a tremendous encouragement to experience at first hand the extent and diversity of contemporary chaplaincy practice. However, the fundamental inspiration for my commitment to chaplaincy practice remains the people who have invited me over the years to come alongside them as a chaplain and to share in their lives. It is those people who have taught me about the enduring value and significance of this collaborative ministry. My heartfelt thanks go to them.

Victoria Slater,
February 2015

Introduction

This book sets out to answer two deceptively simple questions: 'What is chaplaincy?' and 'What is the significance of chaplaincy within the mission and ministry of the contemporary Christian Church?' It does so within a practical theological framework that roots the endeavour in several layers of practice and experience. It is rooted in my own experience over many years as a health-care chaplain, the experiences of chaplains and others involved in my research into the development of chaplaincy in community contexts (Slater 2013), and the experiences of a wide network of chaplains who have generously given of their time in responding to my wider research interest in the ministry that we call 'chaplaincy'.

As I begin to explore these questions, I have in front of me a postcard bearing the image of a chaplain. The image is part of a twelfth-century apse mosaic from the Basilica of Saint Clement in Rome. The man designated 'Il cappellano' bears a tonsure, is dressed in a simple white alb with a girdle and is holding a round vessel, while a curious multi-coloured bird looks on from its perch on a stylized leaf. A scholar of this period may well be able to say a lot more about this image, but, taken at face value, it can speak to us of the continuities and discontinuities of chaplaincy. On the one hand, chaplaincy is an historic form of ministry that some trace back to Martin of Tours in the fourth century (Jones 2010) and his act of charity in tearing his cloak in half to share it with a beggar in need of protection from the elements. The *Shorter Oxford English Dictionary* traces the etymology of the word back to the Old English *capellan* which was eventually superseded by the medieval Latin *capellanus* meaning 'custodian of the cloak of St Martin'. In this period, the term generally referred to a priest of a particular chapel or a chantry priest.

Historically, chaplaincy developed to serve the needs of those who might otherwise be unable to participate in the congregational life of churches either through incarceration or through membership of closed communities in contexts such as education, health, prisons, the military and government. This was the root of the continuing tradition of public sector chaplaincy, jointly resourced both by churches (and more recently different faiths) and organizations and institutions in the public sector. Other roots lie in the engagement with industry and commerce including, for example, industrial mission, international port chaplaincy and agricultural chaplaincy. Again, this tradition extends pastoral care to groups who would otherwise be untouched by the mission of the churches and engages with the life of society (Todd, Slater & Dunlop 2014). Another strand of chaplaincy, rooted in the Middle Ages, is represented by clergy in non-parochial roles who serve particular aspects of church life such as chaplains to bishops, religious communities and possibly cathedrals.

There is then a long tradition of chaplaincy within the Christian Church which changed and developed down the centuries in order to serve the needs of people in particular contexts. On the other hand, if we return to the ecclesiastical location of the Roman image of the chaplain, we might ask what connection the image of a medieval religious person has with contemporary expressions of chaplaincy such as chaplains to the police, retail centres and football clubs. The Roman image is represented against a shimmering golden background above the sanctuary, the Church's symbolic centre of sacred power. This raises the questions: where might chaplains be located and represented within the contemporary Church, how are we to represent chaplaincy today, and, more fundamentally, to what are we referring when we use the term?

Sometimes, an inconsequential thought or aside that someone throws out sticks unaccountably in the mind, its memory activated years later by particular experiences. After nearly 30 years,

I admit to not remembering much about the lectures I attended during my theological training. However, one thing I do remember is Professor Nicholas Lash, Norris-Hulse Professor of Divinity in the University of Cambridge at the time, saying that what really surprised him about theologians was the fact that so many of them seemed to find it so easy to talk about God. These seemed to me then, and still seem to me today, to be wise words. They came back to me when I began to write about chaplaincy because, during the past few years of chaplaincy research, what has really surprised me is the fact that so many people seem to find it easy to talk about chaplaincy without acknowledging the fact that it is not at all clear what we are talking about when we use the term. What does the word signify? What do we actually mean when we use that word today? How can we talk meaningfully and coherently about chaplaincy both within and outside the institutional Church unless we have some level of theological and conceptual understanding of it as an ecclesial practice?

In order to address this issue, this book seeks to describe not only what chaplains do, although obviously that is fundamental to any conceptualization of the practice, but also to consider the nature and significance of contemporary Christian chaplaincy as a form of ministry undertaken on behalf of faith communities.

The research that underpins this book was undertaken in 2011–12, while I was working at the Oxford Centre for Ecclesiology and Practical Theology (OxCEPT), an ecumenical research centre based at the Anglican theological training college Ripon College Cuddesdon. Part of my role was to research ways to develop effective chaplaincy practice in community contexts, and the research represented here was intended to support this remit. As I began to explore chaplaincy in community contexts, it very soon became clear that there was an identifiable trend towards the development of chaplaincy roles across all denominations and a renewed interest in chaplaincy from the mainstream churches. For example, both the Methodist and Baptist Churches had produced their own research reports (Bowers 2005; Culver 2009). What was absent was any substantial consideration of *why* this renewed growth and interest was taking place and what its significance might be within the mission and ministry of the Church today.

A quick glance at the job advertisements in the church press in any week reveals a substantial demand for people for chaplaincy posts. The posts advertised are most likely to be for school, healthcare, the armed forces or prison chaplains, and the number of posts is significant. However, if one's antennae are tuned to the chaplaincy frequency in general, a much more comprehensive and complex chaplaincy profile appears. As a practical theologian and researcher into chaplaincy, over the past five years my antennae have been intentionally tuned in to the field of chaplaincy, and I have picked up something remarkable. Whatever social context I have investigated, I have found some kind of 'chaplaincy' activity. I have found chaplaincy to nursing and care homes, the police, courts, emergency services, the Olympic Games, retail centres, industry, the racing industry, the commercial sector, GP practices, the homeless, sports clubs, mayors, airports, waterways, ports and bus services . . . the list could go on.

Three things are remarkable about what I have found. The first is the extensive social reach of chaplaincy ministry. At a cultural moment when the institutional Church finds it hard to reach the majority of people who may be open to 'God' or a transcendent reality but closed to institutional belonging, chaplaincy seems to be flourishing through its ability to meet and minister with people where they are in the midst of their daily lives. The second remarkable thing is the fact that these chaplaincy roles have emerged so rapidly over the past decade within a diverse and plural social context. The third is that this exponential growth in chaplaincy has hitherto not been identified as a ministerial trend or phenomenon: roles and chaplaincy practice have developed rapidly but there has been little accompanying theological reflection on practice. While research and writing about chaplaincy is developed in certain contexts, most notably healthcare, there is little critical theological reflection on the practice of chaplaincy as a whole and specifically on its significance within the mission and ministry of the Church. In the developing field of chaplaincy studies, the emphasis has hitherto been on the study of institutional chaplaincy such as in prisons, the armed forces and healthcare rather than on roles in community contexts such as nursing homes or town centres or on what is happening from the perspective of the Church. It is the significance of chaplaincy in community contexts within the mission of the Church that is the main focus of this book, though much of what it has to say will resonate with wider chaplaincy practice. The main contention is that chaplaincy is central to the mission of today's Church. This contention is supported with evidence based on qualitative case study research of the development of chaplaincy roles. It is this research that enables the voices of chaplains to be heard and thus roots the argument in practical experience.

The overall picture of the situation of chaplaincy presented above has several profound implications. First of all, because chaplaincy is embedded in social contexts, it is appropriately shaped by the context in which it is practised and therefore every chaplaincy works differently and is, in this sense, unique. For this reason, reflection on chaplaincy has usually been structured around a taxonomy of institutions (Brown 2011, p. 6) such as hospitals and prisons. This in turn has meant that a wider critical reflection on the nature of chaplaincy as a genre of ministry within the Church's economy of ministry and mission as a whole has been neglected. This is not surprising given how daunting a task it is to identify commonalities within such diversity of practice. However, given the situation outlined above, this is now a necessary task, and it is this task that the book addresses.

Critical theological reflection on chaplaincy is necessary for several reasons. First of all, if (and it is a big if) the institutional Church understands its missional vocation as the quest to participate in God's project for God's world and if that quest is its priority, then chaplaincy, in its engagement with people's everyday lives, must have a significant contribution to make to the fulfilment of that vocation. That contribution needs to be recognized within the Church, if chaplaincy is to be appropriately supported, developed and resourced, and if it is to fulfil its potential to contribute to and enrich the life of the whole Church. The rapid emergence of so many chaplaincy-type roles over recent years has resulted in many practitioners doing invaluable work in society but without a developed narrative for chaplaincy to undergird the work and inform the development of best practice. Such a narrative is needed to provide a coherent account not only of what chaplains do and how they do it, but also why they do what they do, a theological rationale for the work. Given that chaplains work in the public square[1] and that they are, in effect, practical apologists for the faith they represent, it is vital that they are able to give an account of the work they do. This kind of narrative could represent chaplaincy both within the Church and to secular organizations that employ or support chaplaincy.

The lack of such a narrative has meant that chaplaincy is not represented within the central missiological and ministerial discourses of the Church. A prime example of the failure of the institutional Church to grasp the significance or potential of chaplaincy in the contemporary cultural context is the omission of any mention of it in the influential Church of England report *Mission-Shaped Church: Church Planting and Fresh Expressions of Church in a Changing Context* (Archbishops' Council 2004). This report has had a pervasive impact on practice and on subsequent discourse about mission within the Church of England. Although the report was criticized for being ecclesiologically conservative, focusing on evangelism rather than mission (Hull 2006), nevertheless it did signal an awareness of the importance for mission of the Church's relationship with the prevailing culture. It represents the start of a process of discernment and adaptation that has led to the idea of a 'mixed economy' of different types of ministry (Bayes & Jordan 2010) including the movement of 'emerging church', Fresh Expressions[2] and Pioneer Ministry (Goodhew, Roberts & Volland

---

1 Understood with Todd (2011, p. 7) as 'those virtual and actual spaces in which public norms and policy are negotiated and enacted for the good of civil society'.

2 Fresh Expressions here refers to the joint initiative of the Church of England and the Methodist Church which supports and resources new ways of being Church alongside traditional churches in parishes and circuits. The Fresh Expressions website can be accessed at www.freshexpressions. org.uk.

2012). The Fresh Expressions website defines a pioneer minister as 'a missionary entrepreneur with the capacity to form and lead fresh expressions and new forms of church appropriate to a particular culture'. All these initiatives represent an attempt to re-enculturate the gospel and to renegotiate the relationship between the institutional Church and society. It is remarkable that neither the report nor subsequent discussions about ministry have mentioned the contribution that chaplaincy makes. This seems to be a startling and somewhat puzzling omission given the extent and social reach of chaplaincy across the generations.

The hiddenness of chaplaincy within church structures and discourse was highlighted in a recent research report for the Mission and Public Affairs Council of the Church of England (Todd, Slater & Dunlop 2014). The report signals the complex nexus of relationships and tensions that exists between chaplaincy ministry, church-based ministry and the institutional Church. An exploration of these relationships will be central to the argument of this book. However, the forging of any kind of healthy relationship requires us to have a sense of our own identity in the first place. If chaplaincy is to enter into genuine dialogue with different ministries within the Church and with secular[3] contexts, it is necessary to have some conceptual clarity about what chaplaincy is. This book therefore must also address the deceptively simple question: what is chaplaincy?

Hitherto, there has been a tendency in chaplaincy literature (Legood 1999; Threlfall-Holmes & Newitt 2011a) to focus on descriptions of practice rather than on an attempt at interpretive analysis that could forge conceptual clarity about the nature and identity of chaplaincy as a genre of ministry. Until there is some degree of clarity about what makes chaplaincy 'chaplaincy' as distinct from other genres of ministry, it is impossible to address the question of its significance for the mission and ministry of the Church.

---

3 I use the term 'secular' in the book to denote that which pertains to civil society rather than the Church and religion.

At present, 'chaplain' is in danger of becoming an umbrella term that can be used to denote anyone from a church with involvement in a secular context. I have known it used to refer to informal part-time pastoral visiting at one end of the spectrum to a formalized 'professional', contracted and accountable service at the other– for example, in a further education college. How chaplaincy is understood is fundamental to how roles in a specific context are negotiated, set up, developed and resourced and to how faithful practice is sustained. Understanding what makes chaplaincy 'chaplaincy' is therefore the foundation for what this book tries to do.

Since the publication of the *Mission-Shaped Church* report in 2004 the debate about mission and ministry in the Church of England has intensified. The Church is in the process of re-thinking what its calling to serve God's mission to the whole of society in the twenty-first century implies for the structures of ministry. Hitherto, the debate has tended to be polarized between those who stress the importance of place and the parish as the fundamental model for ministry (Percy 2008; Davison & Milbank 2010), and those who stress the importance of engaging with culture such as those involved with Fresh Expressions (Goodhew, Roberts & Volland 2012). Chaplaincy has been lost within this debate. A good example of this is the Westminster Faith Debate[4] on the future of the parochial system held in Oxford in October 2014. This asked whether the 'parish church–parish priest' model can survive, and if not, what might take its place. The debate was about appropriate contemporary models of ministry: the contribution that has been made by the development of fresh expressions of church was acknowledged, but there was no mention of chaplaincy until its relevance to the debate was briefly mentioned in a question from the floor.

The emergence of chaplaincy roles in community contexts signals an instinctive ecclesial response to the challenge of cultural change. This response recognizes the complexity of the contemporary plural context and therefore the need to move beyond

---

4 Further information can be found at www.faithdebates.org.uk/oxford.

the polarities of the debate between place and culture in order to make a nuanced response to context. It is the genius of chaplaincy that it finds ways to respond to and flourish in diverse contexts. This capacity, evidenced in the case studies presented in Chapter 2, gives the long tradition of chaplaincy ministry fresh contemporary significance, because it now provides missional opportunities for engagement with civil society that, for a variety of cultural and resource-related reasons, are not easily available to many parish clergy. The number of stipendiary ministers is diminishing, parishes are being combined and many clergy simply do not have the time to spend in the contexts where people live out their lives such as further education colleges, nursing homes or the workplace. Chaplains can and do reach sections of the population that parish ministers find it increasingly hard to reach. Prime examples of this would be the work of school and military chaplains with young people, chaplains to the growing number of elderly people in care, nursing homes and retirement homes, and the work of most chaplains with people who do not espouse a particular faith tradition and/or do not have a connection with a church community.

In this challenging context, a current ecclesiological imperative is to find ways of engaging with the whole of society. At the same time, there is a declining number of stipendiary parish clergy and ministers. It is therefore not surprising that there has been a resurgence in interest in chaplaincy from the churches. For example, the Methodist Church of Great Britain has invested in a major Chaplaincy Development Project and has developed a training course for congregation members called *The Chaplaincy Everywhere Course.*[5] It is perhaps more surprising that in a plural cultural context that accommodates a variety of discourses including militant atheism and religious fundamentalisms as well as disillusionment with religious institutions, particularly in the light of sexual abuse scandals, chaplaincy seems to be holding its own. This is therefore an apposite moment to reflect on the contribution that chaplaincy makes as part of the Church's witness and service in the world.

---

5 The course can be accessed at www.methodist.org.uk/mission/chaplaincy.

The purpose of the book

This book therefore aims to provide a coherent narrative of the significance of chaplaincy for the mission and ministry of the contemporary Church that is rooted in empirical research. It sets out to provide a theological rationale for chaplaincy, some conceptual clarity about what chaplaincy actually is, and practical suggestions for the development and support of chaplaincy practice. This narrative moves beyond the common polarization of 'chaplaincy' and 'Church' to position chaplaincy as a distinctive genre of ministry with its own identity and integrity that, together with other genres of ministry, makes a significant contribution to the mission of the contemporary Church understood as the service of God's mission in the world. I write as an Anglican priest and healthcare chaplain with a background in chaplaincy research, training and education. I am aware of the fact that most chaplaincy takes place within multi-faith and ecumenical contexts, and I work in healthcare in such a plural context myself. However, the context of the research on which this book is based was Anglican ministry, although there was an ecumenical dimension to one of the case studies. This means that the focus of the book is on Christian chaplaincy and the mission of the Church in England. Having said this, the point of the book is to present a story for chaplaincy, and I hope that what it has to say will be relevant to and resonate with the experience of readers and practitioners from a wide variety of denominational, faith and chaplaincy backgrounds.

The structure and approach of the book

Chapter 1 discusses chaplaincy in an historical perspective and in the context of a plural contemporary culture that challenges the Church to find ways in which to engage with the whole of society. Chapter 2 exemplifies the practical theological approach taken in the book by rooting what it has to say in practice. The chapter describes three case studies of the development of chaplaincy roles in community contexts which enable the voices of chaplains to be heard. It provides evidence of how and why particular roles developed, paying particular attention to the relationship in practice between chaplaincy development and theologies of mission.

Chapter 3 goes on to explore in depth the relationship between chaplaincy ministry and the mission of the Church providing a theological rationale for the development of chaplaincy roles. It discusses the fact that once a role is established tensions between chaplaincy and church-based structures of ministry often come into play. It suggests that in order to address these tensions, it is necessary to understand what makes chaplaincy 'chaplaincy'. Chapter 4 therefore addresses this question and discusses the identity and integrity of chaplaincy as a genre of ministry. The chapter provides some conceptual clarity by proposing three dimensions of chaplaincy that can provide parameters within which chaplaincy best practice can be developed and sustained.

Having discussed the distinctiveness of chaplaincy as a genre of ministry, Chapter 5 looks at some of the challenges it presents to the institutional Church, and in particular the relationship between chaplaincy and church-based ministry. It recognizes that the problem of how different ministries relate is linked to the ecclesiologies that are explicitly or implicitly in play within a specific context: different understandings of what the Church is and what it is for inevitably underpin understandings of and attitudes towards different ministries. The chapter draws on the research evidence to explicate the relational dynamics within people's ministerial experience. These findings are then discussed with reference to an ecclesiology of ministry that suggests how chaplaincy could be understood in relation to other ministries and to the mission and ministry of the whole Church. Finally, Chapter 6 returns to practice. The chapter suggests some ways in which the distinctive understanding of chaplaincy described in the previous chapters may be used to develop and support practice. It discusses the need to represent the voice of chaplaincy within current church thinking about the selection and training of lay and ordained ministers, the provision of pastoral supervision for chaplains, and the need for chaplaincy research. It also presents a developmental consultancy model designed to help people who are considering setting up chaplaincy roles.

This book is therefore rooted in a practical theological approach that begins with and returns to practice. Chaplains are located in the structures of society at the interface between the Church and contemporary culture, a location that mirrors that of practical theology in which contemporary experience and the resources of the religious tradition meet in critical dialogue that has the potential to be mutually and practically transforming (Woodward & Pattison 2000). The purpose of this book is therefore consonant with the practical theological endeavour characterized as 'critical, theological reflection on the practices of the Church as they interact with the practices of the world with a view to ensuring faithful participation in the continuing mission of the triune God' (Swinton & Mowat 2006). It aims not only to offer some theological and conceptual insight into current chaplaincy practice but also to be practically useful in the faithful development and transformation of practice.

Who this book is for

The intention is that the book will be useful to those who are engaged in or thinking about developing a chaplaincy role, as well as those who are in a position to support and develop chaplaincy ministry in dioceses and the wider Church. As a worked example of Case Study research, I also hope that it will be useful to people involved in researching practice or who are contemplating doing such research. It is intended for lay and ordained people in ministry, paid or voluntary, who have or are thinking about undertaking a full- or part-time chaplaincy role. In addition, it may also be useful to people who supervise or support chaplains, ministerial students who are interested in exploring chaplaincy ministry or feel that they are called to that ministry, theological and ministerial educators, those engaged in the continuing professional development of ministers, students undertaking studies in chaplaincy, and leaders in mission and ministry. This, of course, may not prove to be easy reading. As we shall discover, there are reasons why chaplaincy ministry has not been on the radar of the institutional Church for so long. Chaplaincy poses to the Church some fundamental challenges including a prophetic, missional challenge to congregations, an ecclesiological challenge to think about the very nature of the Church and its vocation, a governance challenge, and a resources challenge given that for the Church of England at least, its main income is generated in parishes. However, for those of us who thrive on challenges, chaplaincy provides an opportunity to think afresh about how the Church can best engage with the whole of society in the twenty-first century and thereby be faithful to its vocation to serve the mission of God in the world.

The hope is that the practice-based evidence presented here may provide a basis for ongoing discussion and the development of thinking. This does not claim to be a definitive narrative, but rooted as it is in my own and other people's experience of chaplaincy ministry, it is a valid narrative that I hope will at least give a voice to chaplains working in diverse social contexts. I hope that it may also encourage people working in such roles to reflect on the significance of their work within the mission of the whole Church and encourage the Church to think more deeply about the missiological, theological, ecclesiological and ministerial significance of a ministry that may be becoming a more normative form of ministry in the Church than the parochial model (Threlfall-Holmes & Newitt 2011a, p. 139).

During the course of my research, a chaplain to older people said that she thought chaplaincy was 'fine work'. I agree. For example, an elderly man in a hospice day centre always withdrew behind his paper when the chaplain visited and would have nothing to do with her. Having watched the chaplain talking with other people over several weeks, much to her surprise, one week he decided to join a small group of people who had asked for a service to be held. Afterwards, as the chaplain sat and listened, he told her about his wartime experiences; he had been unable to reconcile the human suffering he had witnessed with the existence of a loving God and he had turned away from God. In his anger, confusion and distress he had never had anything to do with religion since. He talked a lot over subsequent weeks, and in the end was able to find some peace and reconciliation within himself and with God before he died. It is unlikely that this person's spiritual and emotional pain would ever have been addressed, let alone alleviated, if there had not been a chaplain embedded in that context. This small vignette points to the missional potential of chaplaincy as an embodiment of the Church in civil society, able to come alongside people in the context of their daily lives and to be, in effect, the Church in practice.

I

Chaplaincy in a Changing World

Introduction

During my career as a healthcare chaplain there have been certain experiences that on reflection can be seen to have been part of a much wider picture than was immediately apparent. Such experiences are necessary reminders of the extent to which our practices and the ways in which we each construct and understand our individual and social reality are profoundly influenced by the prevailing social and cultural context in which we live and work. In thinking about the changing context within which chaplains practise, one particular experience provides a glimpse into the complex cultural space that chaplaincy inhabits.

In the late 1990s, I was working as a hospice chaplain. The hospice charity held an annual event at Christmas called 'Light up a Life', a common practice for hospices across the country. People whose loved ones had died under the care of the hospice in the previous year were invited to sponsor a light on a Christmas tree. This enabled them to write a message of remembrance which was collated into a book of remembrance. The book was kept at the hospice so that people could later return to consult it if they wished. This event was part of the care for bereaved people. The constituency of people served by the hospice was mainly white British; it was not culturally or ethnically diverse. For many people, this provided an opportunity to return to the hospice, often with the support of family and friends, and to be part of a wider community of bereaved people, all of whom were taking time to remember loved ones at what can be a particularly poignant time of year. The sponsorship of the lights meant that the event also raised funds for the work of the hospice. The event was held outside around a large Christmas tree, a Salvation Army band provided the accompaniment for some traditional carols, the local radio broadcast the event to which hundreds of people came, civic leaders attended, and I was asked to lead a short inclusive time of prayer and reflection around the switching on of the lights. During this time of reflection, a period of reverent silence was held during which people could remember loved ones in their own way but as part of a wider group of mourners. The first year went well, and there was a lot of appreciative feedback. Subsequently, a decision was made by the organizers not to have any kind of 'service', however inclusive, as, despite the fact that people would be singing Christmas carols, there was a concern not to exclude anyone. As far as I am aware, this decision was not a response to feedback from participants, which was good, but rather it appeared to reflect the organizers' concern about the place of religion in public life. The compromise was that while the cultural context of the event would remain Christian (singing Christmas carols), all the other input would be secular. The mayor would switch on the lights and say a few words. Following this redesigned event, some of the feedback thanked the hospice for providing the opportunity to remember and commemorate loved ones at a difficult time, but reflected that it wasn't the same without a 'service', something was missing.

This vignette focuses in practice a cultural ambivalence, if not confusion, about the place of religion and its representation in the public square in the context of a plural society. It also raises the question: what was missing? As Swift notes, in spite of the waning of religious authority and the Church's social status in public institutions, there still remains within people 'a longing for something *other* which is persistent and may even be growing' (Swift 2014, p. 135). I suggest that the recognition, representation and response to that prevalent but hard to articulate 'longing for something other' lies at the heart of skilful chaplaincy practice. In order to begin to understand why chaplaincy roles have been growing in both number and diversity over the past decade, this chapter therefore considers the relationship between chaplaincy and the various contexts within which it is located and with which it is in constant dialogue. These contextual perspectives are constantly in play influencing the practice and development of chaplaincy roles. As the vignette above suggests, two of the most salient contextual influences are the relationship between the Church and the prevailing culture, and the rise to prominence within society of 'spirituality' as a widely accepted category of human experience and mode of discourse. People may remain open to the transcendent in human experience but be unwilling to accept any kind of religious authority or accede to propositional beliefs. Whether or not one believes in 'God', the decision to participate in a faith community is a matter of choice, one among many alternatives in a market place that is full of courses, groups, practices and therapies that offer the promise of personal and spiritual fulfilment. The discussion of chaplaincy therefore needs to begin by addressing the wider contextual influences that inevitably shape chaplaincy practice.

The contemporary plural context and the narrative of secularization

Swift (2014) notes that chaplains stand at the intersection between the historic presence of the Church in the public square, secularization, contemporary spiritual expression, and direct engagement with the fundamental realities of people's lives. How chaplains negotiate the occupation of this space is determinative of whether or not chaplaincy will flourish. It is a demanding and complex space to inhabit. As Todd (2011) points out, in the mid-twentieth century, when the National Health Service was founded, one of the underlying purposes of chaplaincy was to extend the ministry of the Church to those who were unable to access that ministry for themselves. This included the sick in hospital and those in prison. As such it was (and remains) part of the churches' engagement with social responsibility and of the involvement of the whole Church in the public square. Underlying this commitment to public engagement was a parochial ecclesiology which understood the Church as existing to serve the whole of society. The Christian Church in this country, particularly the established Church of England, held a privileged place in the life and institutions of the nation. Since that time the norms that govern life in the public square have changed significantly in the light of rapid globalization and increasing cultural, ethnic and religious diversity.

In a recent RSA (Royal Society for the Encouragement of Arts, Manufactures and Commerce) report *Spiritualise: Revitalising Spirituality to Address 21st Century Challenges*, Rowson discusses the contemporary importance of the role of spirituality in the public realm. He refers to the three forms of secularization described by Charles Taylor in *A Secular Age* (2007) stating that the report speaks to the third form of secularization that concerns 'the shared societal conditions of belief in which "belief in God is no longer axiomatic" . . . society's spiritual diffusion means there is no shared touchstone to illuminate the purpose of our lives' (Rowson 2014, p. 10). This broad understanding of secularization points to the plural nature of contemporary society and is one of many in the debate about the nature and extent of this phenomenon. However, as Todd notes, whatever one's view of the secularization debate and the extent of the decline in religious involvement in public life, the norms that govern public life have changed significantly over the past four decades. Social norms have been secularized such that policy and practice are now located within the two main discourses of human rights and diversity of culture and morality. Todd contends that this has established pluralism as a norm: it is seen not only as a fact that society is diverse or as a right so that people are free to be different, but as a good in that diversity is seen as contributing to the wellbeing of society.

The stress on human rights and diversity led to a variety of equal opportunities legislation culminating in the Equality Act 2010, which is intended to protect people against discrimination. The protected characteristics of the Equality Act are: age, disability, gender reassignment, marriage and civil partnership, pregnancy and maternity, race, religion or belief, sex and sexual orientation. Chaplaincy exists within and is shaped by this culture created by the prevailing public norms of human rights, diversity and equal opportunity. In order to flourish in this meta-context, chaplaincy has constantly to negotiate and renegotiate its practice, language and identity while preserving its integrity as faithful practice. This is one reason why chaplaincy can be both challenging and exciting as a form of ministry. It offers the opportunity for the Church to meet people where they are in the midst of the triumphs, tragedies and tedium of daily life and to engage in genuine dialogue with a diverse society. However, at the same time it needs to remain aware of the prevailing social norms within which it practises and of the suspicion or even hostility that can be generated towards religion by the awareness of religious fundamentalisms and religion's capacity for proselytism.

The dialogic nature of chaplaincy

Chaplaincy and the ecclesial context

The kind of chaplaincy practice that is the primary subject of this book is located in the structures of society such as care homes or retail centres. It therefore sits at the interface between the institutional churches which chaplains represent and particular social contexts of engagement. This means that chaplains are not only in dialogue with the prevailing culture but also, to a greater or lesser extent, with the Church they represent. In particular, chaplains who have dual roles as parish ministers or congregation members are in close dialogue with local congregations. Churches, of course, have their own particular institutional and local culture, a term which I understand as referring to the way of life, customs, shared meanings, values and beliefs of a particular group of people at a particular time. This is not unproblematic. While there are examples of good working relationships between chaplains and local churches and within dioceses, the findings from my own research (Slater 2013) and from recent chaplaincy research undertaken for the Church of England (Todd, Slater & Dunlop 2014) uncover a theme consistent enough to be called a narrative of dislocation. Many chaplains did not feel that the Church valued, validated or understood their work in the same way that it did parish or congregational ministry. In my own research, this sense of dislocation, of the purpose of chaplaincy ministry not being understood or valued by local congregations and/or the institutional Church, was articulated even by chaplains who had a dual role alongside parish ministry. For example, a vicar who was appointed to be half-time parish priest and the rest of the time lead chaplain to a town centre, spoke of how difficult it was to have the dual roles because, in spite of explanations about chaplaincy, her congregation expected her to be there exclusively for them.

The findings from the 2014 Church of England research highlighted this theme of disconnection with examples at the local, diocesan and national levels of church life. This was underlined at a national level by the fact that no accurate diocesan or central church statistics for chaplaincy were kept. There were no reliable quantitative data about the number and type of chaplaincy roles that exist, the number of people exercising chaplaincy ministry or about how that ministry is resourced. In particular, there were no reliable statistics for the considerable number of lay and volunteer chaplains. From a survey of all the dioceses, there were 1,415 chaplains reported as known to the Church of England, although a few key dioceses did not respond to the request for information. Comparison with other chaplaincy research that takes account of the extent of lay and volunteer involvement suggests that this is a huge underestimation of the number of people involved in chaplaincy, an underestimation which could be by a scale factor of between ten and 100 (Todd, Slater & Dunlop 2014, p. 20). If that is the case, there could be in the region of 14,000 people involved in chaplaincy solely from the Church of England.

The quantitative data gleaned from dioceses about the number of chaplains did, however, reveal some interesting sets of distributions. One of these was that across all the categories of full-time and part-time lay and ordained chaplains, the majority were paid by an organization other than the Church of England. This seems to indicate a significant investment in chaplaincy by secular employers. This finding highlights the thorny question of who funds chaplaincy which is directly linked with the capacity of chaplaincy to give an appropriate account of itself, what it is and what it contributes, both to a secular context and to the mission of the Church as a whole. No organization will be prepared to resource a service if it is not clear what contribution it makes to its mission, be it secular or religious. This is the practical reason why chaplaincy needs to be able to give an account of itself: at a time of financial stringency, some dioceses have cut chaplaincy provision. On the figures for known chaplains received from dioceses, about 93 per cent of full-time ordained chaplains were employed by someone other than the Church of England (Todd, Slater & Dunlop 2014, p. 17).

There are complex reasons for this actual and perceived disconnection, but what I want to note here is that there does seem to be a dislocation between the theology and concerns of the Church and those of chaplains who work within the social structures of society. Swift (2014) refers to this as 'the silent exile of the chaplains from the central preoccupations of the Church', while a recent report on chaplaincy from the public theology think-tank Theos observes that for faith and belief groups 'chaplains present a huge opportunity for engagement in the public square, and a significant potential asset, but one that seems often tangential to the central mission of these groups' (Ryan 2015).

The reasons for this dislocation will be fully explored in the consideration of the relationship between chaplaincy and church-based ministry in Chapter 5. However, I suggest that one fundamental reason why this disconnection has been perpetuated is that the recent growth in innovative chaplaincy-type roles has far outstripped any theological reflection on practice. One consequence of this is a lack of conceptual clarity about what the term 'chaplaincy' actually means. The result is that it is difficult to engage in dialogue, because parties may be unclear as to what they are talking about or have different understandings which may or may not be explicit and/or complementary. In one example from the case studies, neither the part-time supermarket chaplain nor the manager who appointed her had a clear conception of what it meant to be a chaplain. Many chaplaincy roles, particularly part-time roles, have developed on a pragmatic, entrepreneurial basis: an initial pastoral relationship or involvement in a particular context has presented an opportunity for an individual to develop a certain role. As a consequence, there can be a lack of a cogent theological rationale for chaplaincy that can be represented to and heard by the Church. As things stand, a lot of theological and other resources have been devoted to Fresh Expressions and pioneer ministry, while chaplaincy has largely been left to get on with things by itself in a semi-detached sort of way. An important aspect of this is that in the Church of England, there is currently no specific training available, apart from a limited number of placements, either to those wishing to explore a vocation to chaplaincy ministry during initial ministerial training or to those in parish ministry who have an interest or involvement in chaplaincy. There are, of course, postgraduate degrees in chaplaincy, but not everyone has the time or the resources to undertake lengthy periods of study. Certainly within the Church of England, there is a pressing need for theological reflection on practice to be undertaken if chaplaincy is to find a voice commensurate with its potential missional significance within the Church as a whole. The finding of such a voice would enable it to engage in fruitful dialogue with the institutional Church.

Chaplaincy, the Church and the contemporary cultural context

The growth in chaplaincy-type roles at a time of widespread decline in church attendance and religious observance, described by authors such as Brown (2009), raises the interesting question of what this implies about the relationship of church and chaplaincy ministry with their social and cultural context. Ballard (2009) has suggested that this growth represents one way in which the Church is adapting to the diverse, dispersed and fluid nature of contemporary life. In my own life, I live in one place, work in another and have a variety of work, social and leisure networks. This is the case for many, if not the majority of people who constantly move between different roles, locations real and virtual, and spheres of activity. Geographical locatedness has therefore declined in significance for many people as they have become increasingly mobile and networks have become global: chaplaincy ministry can be seen as one response to this context. It is, in effect, an attempt to express the relevance of the gospel in every context in which we live our lives, an aspect of the re-enculturation of the gospel in contemporary society. In other words, chaplaincy can be viewed as an ecclesial adaptation, perhaps largely unconscious, to the cultural context. The case studies the book goes on to look at will explore the distinctive social and ecclesial location of chaplains in community contexts. Unlike church ministers, these chaplains are embedded in social structures that shape the role. This is important, because as the case studies will show, it is this embeddedness within a particular context in the public square that gives chaplaincy its missional significance.

The perennial task for the Church is to discern how to fulfil its mission in and to the world. In response to the marked demographic, social and cultural changes that have taken place during the past 20 years, the Church has sought to reconfigure itself in an attempt to maintain a place in public discourse and to find ways of connecting with people who choose not to attend church or have anything to do with a traditional faith community. As long ago as 1994, in *Religion in Britain Since 1945: Believing Without Belonging*, Grace Davie drew attention to the disjunction between practice and belief as a characteristic of post-war religious life in Britain. This posed the prescient question, 'If churchgoing in its conventional sense is diminishing, through which institutional mechanisms can those concerned about the religious factor in contemporary society work outside of the church itself?' (1994, p. 107). As mentioned in the introduction, a decade later the Church of England report *Mission-Shaped Church* (Archbishops' Council 2004) recognized the need for the Church to adapt to its context in dialogue with the prevailing culture in order to remain faithful to its mission to discern where God is at work in the world and to join in with that work. Given the recognition of the imperative to engage with the whole of society and for the Church to resist the temptation to turn inwards under financial and cultural pressure, it is therefore not surprising that there has been a resurgence in interest in chaplaincy ministry in parallel with the widespread decline in church attendance. As one part-time supermarket chaplain and local ordained minister starkly observed, 'If the folk won't come to the church building then [church] folk have got to go out to where the folks are.' It may be that the experience of chaplains in relating to different cultures and contexts proves to be a resource that could enrich the Church's thinking and practice at this particular cultural moment.

Because of its socio-cultural location there is a particular demand placed upon chaplaincy to think about what kind of theological approach it is appropriate for it to take towards engagement with the culture(s) and contexts within which it is embedded. This lies at the sharp edge of practical theology where the focus is on praxis understood as practice informed by and informing theoretical reflection. We perform our theology every day through our practice. The task of practical theological reflection on practice is to call the attention of the Church back to the theological significance of its practices and to the frequent discrepancy between what people think and believe they are doing, what they say they are doing and what they enact in practice. It answers the question, 'How do I know what I really believe until I see what I actually do?' (Cameron 2010, p. 1). This book is itself an extended example of theological reflection on chaplaincy practice that brings lived experience and the resources of the faith tradition into critical dialogue in order to bring to awareness the meanings and significance of the practice. It is this process that enables what is good to be affirmed and the discernment of what might need to change or be developed.

A different example could be taken from my own recent experience. At the end of a cathedral service I attended, everyone was warmly invited for coffee in the refectory afterwards. Once in the refectory, I collected my coffee and stood near the middle of the room, I hope with a relatively pleasant and open demeanour. I watched as the regular members of the congregation, after a few passing acknowledgements with a smile, made straight for their groups of friends and engaged in animated conversation. I had a very pleasant conversation with two Japanese visitors who were, like me, 'strangers' in that place. The discrepancy between the importance of a 'ministry of hospitality' that people wanted to and believed they exercised and the reality of the practice would have been a fruitful focus for practical theological reflection. This kind of reflection attends to the 'deep connectedness' of human experience and the Christian theological tradition (Cameron et al. 2010, p. 13). At best, theory and practice can inform each other in an interplay of mutual transformation, but in order for there to be any chance of that process taking place, there has to be awareness of the theological nature of our practices.

This is particularly true in relation to the theological approach that is taken towards the prevailing cultural context. The kind of approach taken will reflect certain assumptions about the nature of mission and the relationship between 'the Church' and society. Faith communities are having to adopt new practices in response to society's changing culture, but those practices will, to some extent, be shaped by and participate in that culture (Cameron et al. 2010, p. 11). Steddon (2010, pp. 11–12), reflecting on missional engagement in a city centre, provides a useful way to think about this. He posits two theological approaches to engagement with culture which could be said to sit at either end of a spectrum. At one end of the spectrum, 'host' theology engages with the cultural context in order to be able to say, 'Come to our place and do as we do.' This approach would typically have the intention of getting people to attend church or at least to become part of a gathered congregation. Towards the other end of the spectrum, 'guest' theology asks the question – and it is significant that it is a question rather than a statement – 'Please may I come to your place and be part of what you do?' Steddon locates chaplaincy within this second approach, understanding it as the Church dispersed within society rather than gathered as the community of the faithful. It is an approach based on respectful listening, beginning with the fundamental theological assumption that God is present and active in the whole of Creation and that it is the particular calling of the Church to discern where God may be at work and to seek ways to participate in God's creative and redemptive purposes. It is a vision of mission rooted in God's initiative, and this calling to serve the *missio Dei* in the world is fundamental to chaplaincy ministry. Chaplains need to acquire the particular skill of interpreting the deepest meanings of the faith tradition in relation to human experience in dialogue with contexts and cultures that may have no understanding or connection with the language, practices or culture of any faith tradition. As we shall see, this is a demanding and complex task within which chaplains need to maintain their own identity and integrity.

Equally demanding is the challenge to interpret and represent insights and understandings from secular contexts to the Church. Steddon notes the theme of dislocation from the Church that has already been mentioned and the fact that chaplaincy, especially in workplace and city centre contexts, may be perceived by the Church as 'marginal' to its work. He calls attention to the importance of perspective when thinking about the location of chaplaincy ministry and suggests that while it may be seen as marginal or liminal by the mainstream Church, that liminality, poised between Church and society, cuts both ways. If, arguably, the Church has been squeezed to the edge of society, 'then what looks to be "on the edge" as far as Church is concerned, may be plumb centre from where civil society stands' (Steddon 2010, p. 26). The kind of approach to ecclesiological inquiry typified by Steddon's observations recognizes the need for genuine dialogue between the Church and its social and cultural context. It values being in dialogue with disciplines such as sociology, practical theology and ethnography rather than generating ideal, traditional accounts of ministry following a blueprint of the Church. In contemporary contexts where the Church is no longer able to engage from a position of inherited privilege, listening and conversation necessarily become major modes of theological and ecclesial engagement, modes that are characteristic of chaplaincy in its engagement with people's lived experience. As Percy (2005) notes, in today's cultural context, theology and ministry depend substantially on the quality of their social, intellectual and cultural engagement for their value as public discourse. Todd (2011) goes so far as to suggest that given that chaplaincy embraces a practical and dialogical mode of engagement with society which the Church urgently needs to adopt, its mode of engagement may in fact be indicative of the future shape of the Church.

The rise of 'spirituality'

The rise to prominence of 'spirituality' as a category of human experience is one of the most significant cultural developments of the past two decades and an important part of the contemporary cultural context that is relevant to the Church and the development of chaplaincy. Spirituality is notoriously difficult to define, although many have done so with the result that it has been viewed by some as a Humpty Dumpty word that means whatever the person defining it wants it to mean. To counter this tendency and help restore to the concept its subversive challenge to contemporary consumerist culture, in the RSA report mentioned above, Rowson makes the helpful proposal that 'Spirituality needs definition, but it doesn't need a definition' (2014, p. 14). He argues as Swinton & Pattison (2010) have done in the context of nursing care, that it is precisely the 'inclusive ambiguity' of the term that gives it its value, 'the value of the term spiritual is that it gives permission to speak of things that are unknowable' (Rowson 2014, p. 16). The term lacks clarity because it is not a unitary concept, but rather 'a signpost for a range of touchstones; our search for meaning, our sense of the sacred, the value of compassion, the experience of transcendence, the hunger for transformation'.

In an historical perspective, Tacey (2012) notes that the term 'spirituality' has radically changed its meaning over the past few decades. It used to refer to monastics, people who were 'very' religious and pursued the appropriation of faith at a personal and inward level, whereas today, people who are 'not very' religious claim the term. Writing on contemporary spirituality, Tacey suggests that spirituality in religion refers to 'the capacity to enter into the core of a tradition and to weld it to experience', while spirituality outside religion refers to 'the capacity to intuit or bear witness to a depth dimension of experience, which has been lacking during the period of high secularization' (Tacey 2012, p. 472). He contends that the contemporary spiritual search is no longer focused on overcoming the self through acts of humility, self-surrender and compassion for others but is now about the *fulfilment* of the self. This focus can lead to the traditionalists' claim that it is narcissistic, which of course it can be, but he contends 'genuine spirituality is the discovery of an objective life within the self, which is akin to what the mystics and visionaries of various traditions call the God Within' (2012, p. 475). People are searching for 'the divine spark' within the personality, the transcendence of ego, by exploring the depth dimension of the personality. It is, in this analysis, about the exploration of 'soul', the Greek *psyche*, or interiority, and people are looking for guidance in this quest for the human experience of God.

The rise in interest in spirituality, and the decline in interest in institutional religion which reflects the movement identified in Tacey's analysis, has been well documented by writers on spirituality such as Lesniak (2005). She notes that any spirituality is embedded in culture and argues that 'spirituality' is conducive to the contemporary temperament, because it attends to lived human experience and is therefore seen as a more inclusive, tolerant and flexible canopy than organized religion or systematic theology under which to pursue the sacred and the mysteries of the human spirit. Under this canopy sits an endless variety of practices such as meditation and mindfulness, alternative therapies, personal therapy of different kinds, personal development courses, yoga and creative retreats.

Lesniak notes that many contemporary spiritual seekers have sought alternative visions of authenticity and meaning and paths of spiritual development, espousing contemplative resources and practices from different faith traditions which enable them to envision and practise an authentic spirituality without church affiliation. This raises the question of the relationship between

Christian spirituality and a culture in which for many, individual spiritual experience unrelated to a particular faith tradition is authoritative and self-authenticating. How the churches understand and engage with this cultural turn from religion to spirituality is important both for chaplaincy and for the mission of the wider Church. This is of central importance in chaplaincy practice given that chaplaincy is characteristically a 'guest' in a secular context and therefore needs to understand and respect the plurality of spiritualities in contemporary culture in order to be able to respond to people's needs appropriately out of the resources of the faith tradition. This suggests that Christian spirituality needs to be willing not only to challenge prevailing social discourse but also to be kenotic, willing to make its home in those elements of the culture that can house Christian faith today. The kind of language used in this endeavour will be crucial. Given the importance of this area of engagement, it is worth considering this cultural development in more detail.

The rise of spirituality has occasioned a great deal of cultural and religious analysis. Paul Heelas (2002) first presented the cultural theory that a 'spiritual revolution' is taking place in that more people now favour the language of 'life-spirituality' based on personal experience than that of traditional religion. This was tested empirically in research undertaken with Linda Woodhead (Heelas & Woodhead 2005) in the market town of Kendal in Cumbria: the research found that traditional forms of religious association were being influenced by and giving way to new forms of spirituality such as alternative therapies. It also found that a key component of types of churches and spiritualities that were thriving was an engagement with personal experience. Heelas and Woodhead concluded that this shift reflects a wider social dynamic: the subjectivization of culture within which sensitivity to inner life and wellbeing has become more important than conformity to any external obligations or dogma. It is essentially an expressive culture. In the ecclesial context, it may be that this is reflected, for example, in the flourishing of both Pentecostal churches and in the revival of the contemplative tradition across denominations supported by movements such as New Monasticism and the ecumenical World Community for Christian Meditation.[1] In the secular context, the growth of the authority of personal spiritual experience divorced from a specific faith tradition has been viewed from a variety of perspectives. In *Selling Spirituality: The Silent Takeover of Religion*, Carrette & King (2005) contended that cut loose from its roots in religious traditions, spirituality has been colonized by a capitalist agenda and has taken over the public space previously inhabited by religion. They suggest that the ethical and social dimensions that spirituality traditionally draws on have been lost and that it now occupies a 'privatized and conformist' space in society.

While there may be an element of truth to this reading, it seems to me that it cannot be a total reading of such a complex situation and that it is unduly pessimistic. However expressed, I suggest that God is already present in the yearnings of the human spirit for fulfilment and fullness of life. In *The Spirituality Revolution*, Tacey (2004) offers a complementary reading of the place of spirituality in contemporary culture from the perspective of depth psychology. This analysis listens to religious traditions as well as different discourses of spirituality and sees the contemporary engagement with spirituality as symptomatic of deeper human concerns: the longing for sacredness and spiritual meaning, that 'something *other*' that was identified as missing from the secular ceremony described at the beginning of this chapter. Like Heelas & Woodhead, he also recognizes that to thrive in the current context, religious traditions need to take account of personal experience which may indeed be revelatory of God's life and work in the world. Tacey (2012, p. 476) points out that many people in the West have turned to an exploration of Eastern spiritual pathways, which have developed ways of exploring the interior domain through practices such as yoga and meditation, while Western traditions have been perceived as being unable to lead people to life-changing experiences. He suggests that people don't want 'God talk' or preaching but an experience of transcendence; they don't want to obey an old moral code but to

---

1 Information about the community can be accessed at: www.WCCM. org.uk.

live a fully embodied spirituality. If religions can understand this, Tacey believes that 'a bridge between contemporary spirituality and traditional religion will be found'. However, he warns, 'The keynote of contemporary spirituality is experience, and traditions that fail to offer a pathway of experience can expect to decline or diminish.'

In Tacey's view, the churches need to focus on revealing the presence of God in the everyday and ordinary by 'offering guidance, support and spiritual discernment in the scattered community' (2004, p. 197). It is an approach to engagement with 'the rise of spirituality' that seeks to discern and understand the deeper movements in society that it represents by engaging in genuine dialogue on the theological presupposition that God may be at work in this upsurge of interest in all things spiritual. Rather than dismissing much of it as superficial or incoherent, the Church may have something to learn from it about human need and the human desire for meaning, purpose, hope and transcendence in life. It is this human need that chaplaincy at its best is skilled at meeting.

Chaplaincy practice exists in dialogue with and in the space between the discourse of the faith tradition and that of contemporary spiritual experience. This is the space that I had to skilfully inhabit in the 'Light up a Life' ceremony mentioned above. The question that has to be constantly lived in practice is how to live and minister faithfully in this context. Recognizing that it is a guest in a particular context, one of the fundamental and complex skills of chaplaincy is to remain continuously aware of the dialogic nature of the role. Because chaplaincy is embedded in social contexts, its challenge and opportunity is to engage in genuine dialogue with the world that God continuously creates and loves. Chaplaincy praxis inhabits a complex space at the nexus of mutual interplay between several contexts, all of which have their own culture and language. In order to be able to live and work in this space, chaplains need to be able to speak the languages of the faith community, the chaplaincy context and society and to understand how those languages interact and influence one another (Todd 2007). Chaplaincy can therefore be characterized as being dialogic in nature, as represented in Figure 1.

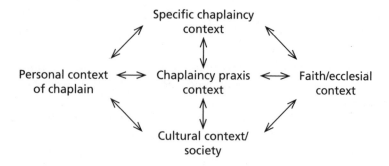

Figure 1: The dialogic nature of chaplaincy.

This dialogic approach to engagement with culture and context is underpinned by a theology of Creation that understands God to be present at the heart of Creation, drawing it into wholeness in Christ (Cameron et al. 2012). This theological stance demands that we pay attention to the world not as 'God's spies' (Muir 1972, p. 188) but as God's co-creators; listening to what God might be saying in *this* context; being open to learn from our encounters with others and, by implication, being willing to change in response to what we learn. This kind of dialogic engagement with the world requires chaplains to have the maturity and humility to remain open to change and emergent insight while maintaining their identity and integrity as representatives of a faith tradition. If that can be accomplished, then a chaplaincy practice stands a good chance of being both faithful and fruitful.

Conclusion

This chapter has presented the culturally engaged, dialogic nature of chaplaincy and the location of its praxis in relation to significant contexts. The exploration of the contemporary cultural context indicates the contours of a subjective, fragmented, fluid and plural social reality which demands an appropriate ecclesial response if the Church is to remain engaged with people's daily lives and a respected participant in conversations in the public square. There are signs that the Church is responding to this challenge as, for example, in the Church of England synod vote to ordain women bishops passed in 2014. I have suggested in this chapter that the officially unrecognized growth in chaplaincy roles in community contexts represents a pre-reflective ecclesial adaptation and response to the challenge of fulfilling its mission to serve the *missio Dei* in the contemporary plural context. Given its social location and the dialogic nature of its engagement with civil society, far from being 'marginal' to the central missiological and ministerial concerns of the Church, chaplaincy needs to be understood as being at the cutting edge of mission, a prime locus of the Church's participation in God's mission in the world for the building up of God's kingdom and the flourishing of all God's people.

Although this exploration may be suggestive of the significance of chaplaincy, such assertions need to be grounded in research into practice. The next chapter therefore presents three case studies of the development of chaplaincies in community contexts that relate the consideration of the contextual background of chaplaincy in this chapter with the reality of practice. This provides the basis for the development of practice-based evidence of how and why chaplaincy roles have developed in ministerial contexts and the relationship in practice of chaplaincy development and theologies of mission. This evidence will then be used to suggest the significance of chaplaincy within the mission and ministry of the contemporary Church.

2

Chaplaincy Development
in a Changing World

Introduction

At a recent conference I found myself talking over coffee with
a parish priest who worked in the centre of a major city. After
telling me about his work, he asked me about my interests. When
I said that I was interested in chaplaincy, he told me that he had
several chaplaincy roles, as he found that this was the most effective way to engage with people in local communities. This kind of
pragmatic development of chaplaincy as a way of enabling missional engagement is typical of the way in which many such roles
develop in ministerial contexts. As previously discussed, the problem is that there has been little, if any, reflection and research into
why so many roles have been developed over the past decade and
what the significance of this trend might be for the mission and
ministry of the Church. Why is it that people like this parish priest
find that taking on chaplaincy roles is a particularly effective way
to engage with people in the public square?

In order to address these questions, I undertook three qualitative case studies of the development of chaplaincy roles in community contexts. This chapter presents the stories of these case
studies which represent the core empirical research that anchors
the book in practice. In view of the fact that the voice of chaplaincy
seemed to be absent from the central ministerial and missiological discourses of the Church, this qualitative research privileged
the voices of chaplains by listening to and representing their

experience and insights. The case studies enabled me to describe and understand what was happening, how the people involved understood what was happening and the processes involved. Because I wanted to understand the significance of this phenomenon for the mission and ministry of the Church, I investigated the practice of Christian chaplains whose roles had emerged in ministerial contexts. Although one of the studies has an ecumenical context, the research focus was Anglican ministry, because this was the primary context of my research practice at the time. However, the findings indicate that these particular stories have a wider resonance that is relevant to the story of contemporary chaplaincy as a whole. For readers who have a research interest or are thinking of undertaking a case study, an account of the research approach and methodology is provided as a prologue to the stories. If you prefer to go straight to the stories, then please feel free to skip the initial section on the research approach. It is the case study stories that provide the basis for the subsequent exploration of the relationship in practice between chaplaincy development and theologies of mission.

The qualitative research approach

The basic elements of qualitative inquiry used in this study include a variety of methods of data collection with people in their natural setting. It is an interpretive approach in which the researcher attempts to make sense of phenomena in terms of the meanings people bring to them. It adopts an inductive approach to data collection and analysis which enables the researcher to describe, interpret and construct meaning and to identify patterns or themes from the data (Cresswell 2007). Because this kind of qualitative research seeks to elicit, identify and develop understandings of the meanings that participants bring to an issue, it is also able to represent the voices of participants and therefore holds the potential to be transformative in enabling certain voices to be heard that otherwise may not have a conduit. In the light of the need there

seems to be to find ways for the voices of chaplains to be represented and heard within the Church, this capacity is particularly
valuable here. The character of qualitative inquiry that I have
briefly described implies a particular view of the world and particular perspectives on truth and knowledge and how they are perceived.
Put very simply, in the positivist tradition of the natural sciences
traditionally there has been a dominant assumption that there is
an objective truth that can be accessed by scientific methods within
which the researcher is detached from the object of the research.
In contrast, qualitative inquiry takes a constructivist approach
assuming that there are multiple realities that are individually and
socially constructed and in which we all participate. The researcher is
therefore inevitably involved in the research process as a participant
and can never be a detached, objective observer. As Swinton (2001,
p. 97) points out, this perspective proposes that '*all* meaning emerges
from the shared interaction of individuals within human society'.

In this view, human beings are constantly engaged in the process
of constructing and interpreting their experience, and the meaning
of any given reality is open to negotiation. This implies that it is
valid to listen to different narratives of human experience, each of
which will be the fruit of a particular process of construction and
interpretation influenced by inter- and intra-personal, cultural and
social factors. This epistemological assumption is particularly apt
to this study with its focus on gathering multiple perspectives and
narratives in relation to chaplaincy and its acknowledgement of
the important influences of personal, social and cultural contexts
to the shaping of understandings and practice.

It is important to say at this point that while it would be possible within this paradigm to adopt the view that all reality is constructed and all truth is relative, this study, located as it is within
Practical Theology, takes a less purely interpretive epistemological stance. Practical Theology is concerned with the discernment
of 'truth', and as a practical theologian I take into account the
claim of the Christian tradition to have received revelation, a
claim that posits a fundamental reality as given and accessible.
As a researcher, I took the view that while there may be many
different perceptions of a particular reality and truth may be

subject-oriented rather than researcher-defined, nevertheless there is a reality that can be accessed, albeit one which is constructed and interpreted in different ways. As the ensuing case studies will show, different narratives reveal different perspectives on the phenomenon called chaplaincy. The assumption in attending to these multiple perceptions is that, taken as a whole, they will bring us closer to an understanding of what reality might look like (Swinton & Mowat 2006, p. 36).

The importance of reflexivity

Within this approach the researcher is unable to stand outside the field of inquiry; he or she is enmeshed in the human process of seeking to make meaning out of experience. There is a recognition that the world-views, values and pre-existing theories of the researcher inevitably influence and shape the research, and the research in turn influences the researcher. A reflexive approach which seeks to make this reciprocal relationship explicit is therefore important in establishing the trustworthiness of the research. This acknowledges the researcher as the primary tool enabling access to the meanings of the issue being explored. She is understood as being integral to the process, bringing unique insights, experience and understandings to the development of knowledge. Reflexivity requires of the researcher constant critical self-reflection 'that enables her to monitor and respond to her contribution to the proceedings' (Swinton & Mowat 2006, p. 59). I am aware that given my own experience, throughout this study I played an integral role as researcher in the generation of knowledge about chaplaincy. For this reason, it was important to be explicit about my own knowledge, experience and understandings of chaplaincy. Openness about this knowledge and experience also enabled me to establish trust and a rapport with participants, the majority of whom were thereby willing to give full accounts of their work experience. I might have got a very different response if I had no experience of chaplaincy and/or held a negative view of the value of chaplaincy within the mission and ministry of the Church.

What is 'case study'? Choosing the case study approach

The use of 'case study' has a long history across disciplines such as medicine, law, psychology and the social sciences. It is often used to refer to descriptions of a phenomenon or situation that is of particular interest or one that holds implications for the development of future practice, a prime example being the development of case law. However, within this current research context it is important to clarify that qualitative case study is something much more complex and methodologically rigorous than the presentation of interesting examples from practice. There is a substantive body of literature about case study by, for example, Stake (1995; 2008), Yin (2009) and Thomas (2011), all of whom identify slightly different kinds and taxonomies of case studies and have slightly different ways of describing what they understand to be the essence of case study. At its simplest, case study can be said to involve the study of a particular issue 'explored through one or more cases within a bounded system' (Cresswell 2007, p. 73). In *Case Study Research in Practice*, Simons's definition captures both the research focus and the action-oriented purpose of case study that is pertinent to this study. This is therefore the understanding that I use:

> Case study is an in-depth exploration from multiple perspectives of the complexity and uniqueness of a particular project, policy, institution, programme or system in a 'real-life' context. It is research-based, inclusive of different methods and is evidence-led. The primary purpose is to generate in-depth understanding of a specific topic . . . programme, policy, institution or system to generate knowledge and/or inform policy development, professional practice and civil or community action. (Simons 2009, p. 21)

By choosing to use a case study approach I have been able to address the two main difficulties encountered in the study of this type of chaplaincy, difficulties which I suspect in some measure account for the dearth of empirical research. The first is that the diversity of context and models of chaplaincy practice mean that it is hard to find a focus of inquiry: on what basis might participants be selected when every chaplaincy looks different according to context? The second difficulty is the related temptation to gather interesting and informative accounts of diverse practice without then taking the necessary step of interpretive analysis in order to inform both theory and practice. This approach enabled me to address the first difficulty by providing a bounded focus for the research. I selected three geographically defined studies that provided contrasting ministerial contexts within which chaplaincy roles had been developed. The choice was geographically based rather than being based on a particular chaplaincy context such as a nursing home or workplace, because the distinctive focus of the research was the development of roles in community contexts which required me to begin with a particular location. The three ministerial contexts were:

1 An Anglican multi-parish rural benefice.
2 A large Anglican team ministry in an urban town centre.
3 An Anglican–Methodist ecumenical project in a semi-urban market town.

The case study approach enabled me to address the second difficulty of moving beyond descriptions of practice to interpretive analysis by enabling me to use a variety of methods of data collection to elicit the different understandings participants brought to the situation. This enabled me to build up a multi-layered description of the complexities of the development of chaplaincy practices in their real-life setting. As well as describing practice, I could capture the processes and relationships involved in the emergence of chaplaincy roles. These were the data that were then available for analysis and interpretation. The methods of data collection that I used allowed both the unique voices of participants to be heard and a set of themes to be developed from a cross-case analysis of the data. The mixture of methods comprised: semi-structured in-depth interviews, the analysis of documents and the collection of information in the public domain, informal observation at meetings, and visits to the contexts. I also kept a reflexive research journal, noting my own thoughts, feelings and insights throughout the process, along with field notes to capture immediate observations, thoughts and impressions after each encounter or interview. The themes that were developed from the analysis are discussed in the next three chapters. They were subsequently explored in critical dialogue with a variety of theoretical perspectives from theology and other disciplines, and with my own understandings and insights as a researcher and practitioner in order to suggest the significance of chaplaincy for the mission and ministry of the wider Church and to develop the implications of the research for practice.

Ethical issues

I have already stated that one of the main issues that this research sought to address was the absence within central church discourses of a chaplaincy voice commensurate with the extent and potential significance of the Church's engagement in this form of ministry. A central purpose of these qualitative studies was therefore to allow the voices of chaplains to be heard. As Denzin & Lincoln (2000, p. 23) note, the interpretive practice of making sense of one's findings has an inbuilt political dimension given that practice-oriented qualitative researchers can 'create spaces for participants (the other) to speak. The evaluator becomes the conduit through which such voices can be heard.' Being transparent about this was part of my commitment to a reflexive research practice. I was aware of this dimension of the role from the start. Both participants and I recognized that the research would be shared with a wider audience within the Church. This meant that the main ethical issues with which I had to deal were consent, confidentiality and anonymity, and participation with its implications about who controls knowledge. One of the difficulties of undertaking empirical research in a church context is that, however much care is taken, it is impossible to guarantee anonymity as someone in church circles is likely to recognize the context. This is particularly difficult given the descriptive nature of case study.

A key ethical dimension of the research was therefore the development of open ongoing relationships with participants. This emphasis on relational ethics (Simons 2009) meant that any issues that arose could be addressed co-operatively through dialogue (Etherington 2007). With this ethical stance I sought to ensure that participants felt able to contact me at any time if they had concerns about the project. Although I made every effort to anonymize the studies and to maintain as great a degree of confidentiality as possible, I made it clear as part of the consent process that I could not guarantee that people would not be identified given that the descriptive nature of case studies may render the location identifiable. None of the participants raised this as an issue. In fact, the majority of participants were eager to tell their story, warts and all. In part, I suggest that this was due to the relational ethical stance of the study. It was important to me that the research process was democratic and that people could participate in the research process. Participants were sent their interview transcripts to check for accuracy and to confirm that they were happy for the information they had provided to be in the public domain. The written case studies were later sent to give people the opportunity to see and to respond to how they were portrayed in the interpreted study. Minor emendations, such as a change of someone's title, were made in response to participant feedback but there were no major difficulties. This then was an iterative process based on relational trust and, as Simons remarks:

It is only in and through relationships in the field, supported by procedures and negotiations over what is fair, relevant and just in the precise socio-political context, that we can *know* if we have acted ethically in relation to those who are part of our case. (2009, p. 110)

A large amount of data was collected across the three studies which provided the material for a thematic analysis (Braun & Clarke 2006), a method for identifying, analysing and reporting

patterns or themes within the data in relation to the main theoretical concerns of the research. The propositions and arguments
that I will go on to make about chaplaincy are made in relation
to the themes I identified through this inductive thematic analysis.
The three themes identified were:

1 The role of theologies of mission in the emergence of chaplaincy roles.
2 The identity and integrity of chaplaincy as a genre of ministry.
3 The relationship between chaplaincy and parish-based ministry.

The stories narrated in the rest of this chapter were written following the thematic analysis.

Before I narrate the case study stories, one final issue concerning
case study needs to be addressed; this relates to how the value of this
type of qualitative research is understood. The primary purpose
for undertaking a case study is to effect an in-depth exploration
of the particular characteristics of that unique case. This means
that the approach rests on the production of idiographic knowledge; that is, knowledge discovered in unique, non-replicable
experiences that is nevertheless presumed to hold meaning and
value. This kind of knowledge is fundamental to both qualitative
research and practical theology (Swinton & Mowat 2006, p. 42).
Idiographic knowledge contrasts with nomothetic knowledge in
the positivist tradition which is replicable, for example in clinical
trials in medicine, so that findings can be transferred from one
context to another. Because case study findings relate to unique
situations, the question of whether and how findings in one situation can be used in relation to different situations has to be
addressed. However, while the findings in one context are not
directly transferable to other contexts, they can resonate with the
experiences of others in similar contexts, offer insights and raise
issues that have significance beyond the particularities of the case.
In this research, I have therefore been able to use an interpretive hermeneutic to develop theoretical propositions based on the
findings that can be tested in different chaplaincy contexts. The
cross-case analysis that I undertook has enabled me to suggest a

theory about the significance of the growth in chaplaincy roles which can be tested beyond these initial studies and therefore, potentially, holds a wider significance. I hope that this testing out will be done. I have recently come across instances of the development of chaplaincy roles that suggest that the outcomes of this initial research would stand up to such testing.

The question of generalization or the wider significance of case study findings crystallizes the rich potential at the heart of case study: the more in-depth the exploration of the particular, the greater the potential both for the discovery of something unique and the recognition of a universal 'truth'. Simons represents this paradox as 'in-depth particularization – universal understanding' (Simons 2009, p. 167). The aim in this perspective is 'to try to capture the essence of the particular in a way we all recognize'. The analogy is with all truly creative art. Think of Shakespeare's *King Lear*, a late Rembrandt self-portrait or Beckett's *Waiting for Godot*: it is through the study of the unique case that we gain insight into the universal human condition.

This relates to the question of how case study can be useful in policy decision-making and the development of practice. As Simons (2009, p. 167) notes, the capacity of case study to present multiple perspectives through a direct encounter with whatever is being studied offers opportunities for policy-makers to increase their understanding of a complex social reality which can then inform the policy decisions they need to make. In this case, those decisions would relate to the development and support of chaplaincy ministry as part of the mission of the Church.

The Rural Benefice Study: The development of an agricultural chaplaincy role in a multi-parish rural benefice

The context

Chris is the self-supporting vicar of a rural benefice comprising four parishes and five churches. She is a retired farmer who trained for ordination after spending most of her life as a livestock farmer in the same village in which she continues to live and minister. The largest parish has 1,400 inhabitants and the smaller ones around 300 each. Chris holds several key roles within the benefice and in relation to the farming community, a situation which has grown out of her embeddedness in this particular context: she knows the local farming community well. Originally a curate in the benefice, she took on the diocesan role of rural life officer, when it became vacant, with the remit to advise the diocese and parishes on rural issues. The Area Bishop gave her a five-year licence to the post. This means that Chris is authorized by and accountable to the bishop in this work and has permission to minister to the farming and rural community not just in the benefice, as would be the case if she were only a vicar, but across the whole of the diocese. She is aware of the potential reach of her ministry across parish boundaries, which means that liaising with local clergy and maintaining good working relationships across the diocese are important aspects of her work. As well as being a vicar and rural life officer, Chris is also a chaplain and regional co-ordinator for Farm Crisis Network, a charity which provides a helpline and volunteer support to the farming community.

The development of an agricultural chaplaincy role

Chris has developed the chaplaincy role as part of the rural life officer post in the context of organizational change. Originally, the rural life officer post was a half-time paid diocesan advisory post, managed within a diocesan department and undertaken alongside a half-time parish role. According to Chris, there was no chaplaincy dimension to the role. This arrangement was discontinued in a diocesan reorganization, and the post is now line-managed by the Area Bishop. When Chris took on the role as a self-supporting minister, she spotted an opportunity to develop a different focus to the role and to develop half of it as chaplaincy to the rural community. Although Chris did produce a suggested job description for the rural life officer, this has never been formally adopted, and consequently there is no role description or contract detailing the amount of time designated for the chaplaincy work. This means that the work is not strategically embedded in the organization but remains an individual entrepreneurial ministerial response to the perceived needs of a particular community of people. Although the bishop authorizes Chris to represent the Church and to develop this chaplaincy work, it nevertheless remains hidden within the institutional narratives of ministry. This means that the grounds on which the work would be accounted by the institution were Chris to leave the role are unclear. There is no explicitly articulated theological or ecclesiological rationale for the chaplaincy work that would enable it to command resources.

Chris has taken on the parish, rural life officer and chaplaincy roles incrementally, and she sees them as having evolved organically as a response to particular circumstances and opportunities. On one level, the agricultural chaplaincy role is presented as a personal initiative, and Chris recognizes that her own experience and personality have been strong determinants of the shape of the role. She remarks of chaplaincy roles in general: '. . . everybody has their own take on it – it's people's personalities that evolve the role, I think'. The fact that Chris has been an integral part of the farming community for many years is fundamental to how and why the role has developed in the way that it has. She knows and is known by this community, and this strong relational base to the work, grounded in mutual trust and respect, is seen by Chris as fundamental. As she says, 'It's because they know me as a farmer that they will talk, they know that I would understand.' It is this strong empathy with the farming community, its struggles, joys and sorrows, that drew Chris to offer to take on the role after she was ordained. For Chris, farming and faith have always been bound together, and this is reflected in her work as an authorized minister. Her ecclesiastical authority to minister is conferred by her ministerial training and formation and the fact that she holds a bishop's licence, but her location as a chaplain within the social structures of the farming community and her solidarity with that community are seen as being equally and essentially the source of her authority by the members of the farming community with whom she works.

Chris occupies three authorized church roles within a particular ecclesiastical and geographical area. This means that there is a substantial degree of overlap between the roles so that there are times when she is 'not quite sure which hat I have on'. This blurring of role boundaries is a marked feature of her work, underscored by the fact that there is no chaplaincy role description. Given the amount of work these roles represent, it is not surprising that managing the available time can be a challenge. It is also the case that because Chris doesn't work in a team, any tension there may be between the parish and chaplaincy work is experienced and expressed in terms of time management rather than in terms of role boundaries and expectations. When there is a conflict of demand, the parish work comes first. At the heart of this complexity sits the fact that there is no role description for the chaplaincy work. This raises the question: what does the chaplain actually do and what does being a chaplain enable her to do that she would not otherwise be able to do as a parish minister? A description of the central components of the role is needed in order to answer these questions.

What does the chaplain do?

As a chaplain, Chris sees herself as having a ministry to farmers which is 'mainly a listening role'. In order to fulfil this ministry, she attends the stock market every week where she is available to offer practical and pastoral support. If people have a particular problem causing stress or anxiety, she may help by liaising with support organizations like Farm Crisis Network. She notes that 'because I understand the problems and I've dealt with them myself for years that is something that I'm trusted to do'. This high level of trust that is foundational to the work is the fruit of the establishment of a broad base of good relationships built on listening, empathy and understanding. From this has grown work with the occasional offices of baptisms, weddings and funerals for which she gains the consent of the parish priest if those involved are from another parish. In general, she is a distinctive Christian presence within and for the farming community, engaging with their everyday lived experience and meeting them where they are both geographically and personally. Because she is a trusted presence, she is also able to respond effectively in times of personal or communal crisis, such as the outbreak of serious disease like Foot and Mouth. As Chris says, 'It's being alongside people so that you build up a trust, so that the trust is there when you need it'; 'being alongside' is seen as fundamental to the work. In this instance of chaplaincy, the wider involvements with structural and policy issues that are part of the chaplaincy role in different contexts are engaged with through Chris's other roles.

The characteristics of chaplaincy

For Chris, the chaplaincy role is specifically characterized by its location within the social structures of the farming community rather than within those of the Church. She sees her role as embedding herself in the farming context in order to be alongside people in the midst of their daily experience of life. She sums this up saying 'The only chapel that I've got is the tea room at the farmer's market.' Although some farmers do attend church, most of the people she works with as a chaplain do not. She is only able to engage with the whole of this community because she has a mandate as rural life officer to work across parish boundaries enabling her to engage with farming networks and to be present where farmers live and associate. In other words, she is able to go to where people are rather than expecting them to come to where the parish church is located. This relates to her perception that the role affords a greater degree of freedom than the parish role to engage with the everyday lives of people and to respond flexibly to situations. Rather than the structures and set duties of parish ministry such as meetings and set services, 'You go with the flow . . . you go where you're led almost.' Chaplaincy is seen as being much more like improvisation than the recital of a specified and rehearsed repertoire and as therefore requiring particular attitudes, qualities, experience and skills. In this role, engagement is continuously shaped by the people or situation with which the chaplain is involved. While Chris enjoys this freedom and the entrepreneurial opportunities that the work brings, she recognizes that it also brings challenges. It challenges her constantly to discern and grasp opportunities for engagement, and at a deeper level it challenges her to work in faith and trust that her Christian presence and witness are fruitful without necessarily knowing how. Chris points to this hidden apophatic dimension of the work when she says '. . . you don't quite know what seeds you're sowing . . . and you don't know what they're going to grow into'.

Chris has a multivalent identity as a parish priest, diocesan officer, chaplain and farmer. She is skilled at utilizing these identities and at moving between different cultural milieus in order to minister appropriately in a given situation. Working as a chaplain outside church structures and networks and to a large extent with people who are not familiar with church culture or with the Christian tradition requires different gifts and skills from those required when working within church structures. However, Chris has had no training for the chaplaincy work. Her expertise, born of experience, remains largely unexamined and unarticulated, and she cannot envisage any training being appropriate to the work: 'I think mainly because I've always farmed and I've had a faith . . . it's just grown out of that . . . I think it would be difficult to have any training.' The role is perceived as being instinctive, and there is no context in which implicit knowledge and skills can be explicated and shared with others so that practice can be developed more intentionally. This also means that there is no explicit narrative about chaplaincy that can represent the work to others at a strategic, institutional or policy level.

Chaplaincy and the mission of the Church

The chaplain is understood by Chris to be a representative Christian person, and she wears a clerical collar as a sign of this identity. She reflects that because of this, people can expect her to be 'quite theological', but because most of the farmers know her as a farmer first and foremost they 'see me as more of a practical person which gives them the security to open up'. She is present explicitly as a Christian minister, and she understands the chaplaincy work as part of the mission of the Church. However, in the interview, Chris was careful to describe what she meant by 'mission', being clear that it is not about getting people to come to church but rather: 'It's bringing God into people's lives at a time when they are vulnerable without ramming it down their throats . . . it's bringing the understanding of God into their problems by what I say or do.' Because she understands the context from the inside, Chris also understands that in order to engage with these people, she needs to communicate 'the understanding of God' in a language, both word and deed, appropriate to the context. This means that the theological underpinning of the work is often not articulated explicitly in the language of the Christian tradition. She quotes St Francis's saying in support of her approach: 'Preach the gospel at all times, if necessary use words.' Mission is here characterized as 'being alongside' people in their daily lives, listening and seeking to understand and discern where God might be at work in those lives in order to be able to respond in a way which bears witness to Christ and contributes to human flourishing and thereby to the flourishing of the Kingdom of God. The language of faith and the Christian tradition mostly remain implicit, the main context in which they are used explicitly being baptisms, weddings and funerals.

Nevertheless, a theological undercurrent runs throughout the work as ordinary everyday encounters are shaped by the theological understandings that Chris brings to them. Not surprisingly, she understands Creation as the main theological theme underpinning the work, saying: '. . . when you see new life born every spring . . . you can't help but be conscious of theology, of Creation, and most farmers would never in a million years articulate that but they're doing it . . .' This links back to the hidden dimension of this ministry discussed earlier, of not knowing what seeds are being sown. The examples Chris cites are of talking to people who unexpectedly refer to words she used at a funeral a couple of years previously or the farmer who was 'not a man of faith' who asked her to go and say prayers because he felt there was 'something evil on his farm'. Such things can happen only because of the relational trust and respect that has been built. In this context, most of the time mission bears the essential character of implicit gracious gift or, as Chris described it, 'It's always an unspoken . . . gift of faith that hopefully I might be able to bring into a situation.'

The case study story

This study shows how, through the exercise of different secular and church roles, a minister embedded in the farming and rural context has been able to discern the need for and the opportunity to develop an agricultural chaplaincy role. This role enables her to come alongside farmers as a representative Christian person to offer support and pastoral care. It shows how the role was developed and is sustained as an individual personal initiative in response to a perceived need rather than having a recognized strategic place within church structures or the institutional narratives of ministry. It shows how comprehensive and complex Chris's involvement in the context is, describing the consequent overlap of roles and the blurring of boundaries. Because of this comprehensive involvement, there has been no imperative to delineate what the narrative for chaplaincy is in this context. This is reflected in the fact that there is no role description and no specified hours in which the work is to be undertaken. This means that the role cannot be represented in terms of the Church as an organization, hence the lack of a strategic or organizational presence. The hidden nature of the chaplaincy is underscored by the fact that there has been no specific training for the post. As a consequence, practice remains within the parameters of individual experience. There is no context in which that experience can be explicated and shared with others in a way which could develop and refresh practice and enable ways to be found of describing the work so that it can be represented to others and developed more intentionally.

The chaplaincy role gives Chris the freedom to work outside church-based structures and across parish boundaries, something that it would be impossible to do as a parish priest. Chris is a highly respected Christian presence within the farming community and she herself values the chaplaincy work highly as part of the mission of the wider Church. However, the role theoretically occupies only one-third of her time, the traditional paradigm of parish ministry remains dominant and its demands on her time take precedence over the chaplaincy work.

The Town Centre Study: The development of chaplaincy roles within a town centre team ministry

The context

The context for this study is a large Anglican team ministry, which covers an ethnically diverse town of about 93,300 people. According to the 2011 census, the three largest ethnic minorities in the district are: Asian/Asian British: Pakistani (7.6 per cent); White: Other White (4.4 per cent); Mixed/Multiple ethnic group (2.8 per cent). There are six Anglican churches in the team with different theological emphases, all seeking to engage with the complex plural context in which they are now set. The team covers areas of deprivation as well as more affluent neighbourhoods. It includes a wide variety of ordained and lay ministers including ordained local ministers, youth workers, a pioneer minister, readers and pastoral workers. The team rector is based in a church in the centre of the town surrounded by large retail centres and drawing its congregation from the surrounding area. Within the team there is a 'mixed economy' (Archbishops' Council 2004, p. xi) of church life, and it is within this diverse missional, ministerial, ecclesiological, religious and cultural mix that chaplaincy roles have been developed. The team has a strategy for mission and the study begins by describing the team rector's perspective on the place of chaplaincy within this strategy before describing the perspectives of practising chaplains. The study looked at five part-time chaplaincy roles that had been developed within the team: lead town centre chaplain; community missioner and police chaplain; supermarket chaplain; chaplain to a charity for homeless people; YMCA chaplain.

Chaplaincy development within the team mission strategy

Paul, the team rector, traces one impetus behind the development of chaplaincy roles to a prayer initiative that began two decades previously when certain members of the congregation began to pray regularly for the town and for the Church to make connections with the people in it. This initiative is seen as having born fruit in recent years and chaplaincy is seen as having played a key part in that flourishing. This missional intention to make connections with people beyond the church walls and to find ways of engaging with them in the midst of everyday life is a key component of the team strategy as described by Paul and of his view of chaplaincy within that.

The second impetus cited is the publication of the Church of England report *Mission-Shaped Church* (Archbishops' Council 2004). Paul views this as having given him a framework to work from in developing a team strategy and places it in the context of what he understands to be the missional character of the Christian faith saying:

> Christians need to feel sent, I mean we're a missional religion: God sends and I think we need to feel sent and in a sense, what I'm saying about the strategic work of chaplaincy and the team is that we were crystallizing that sent-ness . . . Chaplaincy plays to that because it has a significant pastoral focus but also a missional focus too – going out and sharing the love of God and the good news of Jesus Christ with the people around.

In this case, chaplaincy development is intentional, seen as a way of engaging missionally with the town and people beyond the walls of the church and beyond 'ordinary parish life'. When he took up the post, Paul thought there needed to be a culture change in church life in the town centre from what he saw as a fairly passive, church-centred focus to a more active, engaged one. He conceptualizes this shift as the need to move from a Benedictine to a more Franciscan model of engagement. He sees the Benedictine model as one which stresses offering hospitality and inviting people to 'come and join us', a model with which Anglicans are comfortable. He suggests they may be less comfortable with the more peripatetic Franciscan 'Let's go over there and start praying and see what happens.' Paul thinks they are more Franciscan now, 'so the two traditions work together'.

Paul discerned that what was needed was not just 'a benign pastoral presence' in the community but an active engagement with local businesses and community initiatives. The decision was therefore made to appoint a Community Missioner to work in the town centre. That work had developed in various ways over recent years so that there is now engagement with the police service through chaplaincy and with local shopkeepers and retail managers through the town centre chaplaincy team. Paul sees this shift in culture as having 'unquestionably' impacted on church life and the way that congregations now see their ministry.

This is demonstrated, for example, by the fact that congregation members from several of the team churches are now team members in the various ministries such as the town centre chaplaincy. In Paul's view, making connections with people *beyond* ordinary parish life, people who will probably never attend church, is seen as a valued and key characteristic of chaplaincy work, in contrast to parish ministry where most time is spent making connections with people *through* parish life. He believes that the intention of chaplaincy is to be a distinctive Christian presence in a context, enabling people in their daily lives whether or not they are Christians. This is seen as a way of living out authentic discipleship, demonstrating to people outside the church community that 'what we *say* about ourselves is lived out incarnationally, that we actually do go out and show people the love of God in Christ where they are at work and to affirm that work that they do'. Congregation members work in many contexts, but the distinctive thing about chaplaincy is that 'it's a visible sense of that presence', part of an 'incarnate church', 'God just didn't give us the idea of incarnation, he actually sent his Son to demonstrate it, and in a sense, that's what chaplaincy is living out.' Paul suggests that 'people just sense that you stand there for God and there's something quite profound about that in people's lives'.

Paul draws on his own experience as a part-time hospital chaplain to reflect on how a chaplain's relationship with a context or institution is different from that of a parish priest who may visit from outside. He reflects that unlike a parish priest, a chaplain is embedded in the context, knows it inside out and works alongside people as a colleague. However, this embeddedness in a context raises the question of the relationship both with the context and with the Church. Paul is aware that there may be significant tensions here, and his understanding of this has influenced his approach to making chaplaincy appointments:

> I think one of the great tensions for all parish clergy is we can end up running the show and forgetting that we're also called to be out in the world but I think chaplaincy . . . faces the reverse tension . . . you can see a situation where you could actually become almost comfortable being out in the world and so resistant to what the Church is for and about that you live your life entirely on the margins.

In the light of this perception, he considers it important to appoint to chaplaincy roles:

> people who have a very distinct sense of calling to a missional chaplaincy type role but equally who value the life of the Church and want to actually have some significant part in the worshipping life of the community and having a spiritual base themselves.

This rationale for chaplaincy appointments lies behind the fact that the two people in the team with lead chaplaincy roles, the town centre and community missioner and police chaplains, are both also team vicars. Paul sees it as important that they are of incumbent status, saying 'We've given the incipient authority to the role by actually making them priests of incumbent status within the team.' In this view, chaplains are seen as needing to be embedded in a church context in order for their roles to have authority within the team. With this in mind, the study now turns to consider the perspectives of the practising chaplains.

Lead town centre chaplain

The idea for this chaplaincy took shape following an inter-denominational meeting of Churches Together in the town which considered how to maintain a Christian presence in the retail centre given that 'the people don't come into the churches'. Recognizing that there was a substantial Muslim population, it was felt that 'we needed to be out there, be with the people, regardless of creed or colour'. The group prayed about the situation, the idea of a chaplaincy took shape and the hope is that people of different faiths will eventually join the team. An interregnum in a small parish in the team where a third of the population is Muslim led to the decision to appoint someone for two days a week as town centre chaplain and the rest as team vicar.

Kate was appointed to the roles, and as lead chaplain she co-ordinates a team of ten volunteers who each work for two hours a week. She also works with managers of two retail centres, the town centre management, Shopmobility, which facilitates public access, and the police. Volunteers each have an area of operation so that they can build relationships, the idea being that 'the chaplaincy is there to support and walk alongside as a listening friend all who work in the shops, whatever denomination, whatever faith they are'. Volunteers are nominated by their church leader and are given initial training. The work is supported by a group of Trustees, drawn from local churches and Shopmobility, which meets regularly. There is an AGM, and an annual report is widely distributed along with information leaflets about the service for people in shops and for potential volunteers.

Although Kate is an experienced parish priest, she knew before she began training that she wanted to be a chaplain. Prior to ministerial training she had been a Religious Education teacher. She perceived that people 'don't go into churches any more', and she began ministry as a school chaplain. Kate recognizes that for many Church is an alien culture and environment and that there is a big gap between the 'unchurched', who have never had a relationship with the Church, the 'dechurched', who no longer have a relationship, and those who are regular worshippers. She sees chaplaincy as one of the ways to bridge that gap, believing that 'we have got to get out there and show them that the Church is different'. The model she cites for this are the stories of Jesus meeting people in the midst of their daily lives, although she recognizes that a chaplain in the retail park is 'a guest on their ground', invited in by the management team and not there to evangelize. Chaplaincy is understood as being part of mission because 'you're sent out', but it is something more, 'It's actually showing the compassion of Christ . . . in a way that's not always seen in a church setting.' It is seen as a necessary way of taking out the gospel message, a way of walking with people who do not know the stories of Jesus and have no connection with the Church, and it may be that something the chaplain says might spark an interest that the chaplain him- or herself will never know about.

For Kate, chaplaincy is meeting people where they are and walking alongside as a 'listening friend'. This pastoral availability holds the potential for deep encounters as people are willing to share things that it would take a long time for them to be willing to share in a church setting. On the streets, it happens because 'you're on *their* turf . . . their territory, they're more relaxed and you're seen as a friend'. In the interview, Kate spoke of the different perceptions and expectations people had of her in her different roles. She is aware that, as a chaplain, she doesn't have church structures and liturgical roles to work within, so 'It's very much your personality that's out there.' People have their expectations but more perhaps as a person than as a priest or a chaplain, and they are perhaps 'more accepting of what you give them because they don't have the same expectations'. Kate reflected that, unlike in parish ministry where there are set things to do, chaplaincy is characterized by a much more fluid, entrepreneurial response predicated on the capacity to meet people where they are. There are days when the shops are busy and conversations are few, and she wonders what she's accomplished, 'But you've been there and that's the main thing.' At such times, the challenge of the work is to faithfulness so that, over time, the chaplaincy presence becomes recognized and established.

This is also seen as being the case in relation to the churches. As a school chaplain, she felt that her church colleagues did not accept her as a 'proper priest'. In her present role, it has been a challenge to convince colleagues that the work is worthwhile given that the impact is not measurable in institutional terms. She perceives that support from colleagues has grown as chaplaincy has become recognized as part of the economy of church life in the town, but she still thinks the Church is slow to recognize the value of chaplaincy other than in hospitals. This is mirrored in her own parish where she finds tying together the two roles difficult. She perceives that parishioners think the two roles don't sit well together, 'They think they should have a priest to themselves.' This has led her to wonder if there would be more opportunity in the town centre if there was a full-time chaplain and to feel that 'the way ahead for the Church lies in more investment in the chaplaincy roles, right across the board'.

Community missioner and police chaplain

Jenny identifies the impetus behind the development of this role as the recognition by the parish that it needed to engage more fully with the market place in which it was set. A previous rector had a passion for 'going out on the street and meeting people where they were'. The parish wanted to build on this vision for missional engagement, and therefore Jenny was employed as someone with an entrepreneurial approach who was ready to 'get out there' on the streets and build relationships across the town. She is also a team vicar. She was licensed for seven years and was given carte blanche in her community-based role to develop the work. As relationships developed, so involvement in community organizations grew, until she realized that the job was too large for one person. In response to this realization, she developed the vision for a town centre chaplaincy in order to meet the need that she uncovered. Because they have similar ministries, Jenny, the town centre chaplain and the town evangelist work together and support each other as like-minded colleagues, whereas with church colleagues 'chaplaincy is very often looked down upon'. Although the whole ministry team meets once a month, Jenny's experience is that people mostly just get on with their own work. There are certain church colleagues who do recognize and respect the distinctive nature and value of her chaplaincy work. When she was appointed team vicar, she was gratified that one church colleague expressed concern that she was 'possibly going to be spoiled by conventional ministry'. Jenny doesn't think that this has happened, and she is clear that her ministry will always be community-based rather than church-based.

Her real concern is that there should be a distinctive Christian presence at the heart of the community, available to people in their ordinary, everyday lives. She cites the example of Jesus going out to be with people where they live and work and sees the vocation of the Church as following that example. The vocation is to expose ourselves to risky situations, to enter into genuine dialogue with people and potentially 'to have *our* stereotypes bowled over, and also people on the street, to have *their* stereotypes bowled over'. The role of community-based ministry is seen as one of 'calling the Church to account', challenging its ministers to go out to where people are rather than staying in church buildings and culture. For Jenny, this model of engagement is based on the conviction that 'the sacred centre is wherever God is', and as God is everywhere, our prayer must ask, 'Where do you want us to be?', and then we must be prepared to follow where God leads. Christians must be prepared to get alongside people and to listen in order to be able to discern where God might be at work in their lives and to bear witness to their faith. In Jenny's perception, 'There is a lot of faith and spirituality out there', and her role is to gently offer some shape and substance to that and to 'speak for the . . . truth which is within us'.

For Jenny, the essential things are to listen carefully and to underpin action with a well thought out theology. The theology derives from Jesus' example of going out to meet people and it has to be content with mobility. She believes that the Church needs to take courage from this and not be afraid of getting 'up close and personal' with people. It needs to become less introverted and able to be 'invigorated by a fairly foreign environment'. Her view is summed up in her observation that, 'essentially it's about a God who goes . . . it's never really about our mission, it's about God's mission expressed through us'.

Jenny's role as a police chaplain is different in that there she is invited into the institution and has the sanction of the hierarchy. She is accountable to the police, has access at every level of the institution and is expected to be a 'critical friend' who will challenge behaviour as well as provide pastoral support. She believes that what counts is authentic discipleship which leads people to want to ask questions and that both these roles require the living out of faith in the public square: 'It's about challenging the private, public, personal boundary; it's about asserting the sovereignty of God in any situation; it's about setting up mission as life, not just something we do on occasion.' In this sense, chaplains are very much public theologians.

Chaplaincy within a charity for homeless people

Stuart is a team vicar who has been involved with a Christian charity for homeless people since its inception in 2006 and who is currently a Trustee. One of the struggles for the organization has been to understand how the faith that motivated the work in the first place remains integrated in the organization as it develops. Stuart became chaplain because he was ordained and integral to the organization, but it was not until he became a team vicar and had to step back from involvement in the charity that he had time to reflect on the role. He came to the conclusion that there is a choice to make: either to detach himself from current involvement in the organization in order to be chaplain or for him to continue as a Trustee and to appoint a separate chaplain.

This perceived choice arises out of Stuart's growing understanding of chaplaincy. He believes that the chaplain is there for everybody attached to the organization. The role is not church- or denomination-centred, although any chaplain will bring that background as part of who they are. It is for people of all faiths and for those who don't espouse a specific faith. In his view, the chaplain would be a member of the organization but would not be the head of it as a minister in a church would be, and therefore, ideally, he or she would be approachable by anyone. Having a chaplain would strengthen the Christian ethos of the organization, performing a clearly identifiable faith role within a faith organization and being available to look after the spiritual needs of all those involved. The chaplain would be part of the organizational structures and may have input into decision-making processes, but they would not have an executive role. The aim is to be a distinctive presence at the heart of the organization, a relationship summed up for Stuart in the phrase 'integral but detached'.

Stuart sees the chaplaincy work as being about the intensity of real encounters with people, and he sees Jesus as providing the model for this work: 'The model that Jesus gives I think is the model of a chaplain . . . meeting people where they were and when the opportunity arose to talk to them about spiritual things.' The distinctive qualities are having the freedom to go out to meet people, seeking to understand people's context and having a focus for ministry which for Jesus is seen as being 'a kingdom focus'. Stuart believes chaplaincy to be integral to the mission of the Church but that it is a gift or calling to which not everyone is suited. Specific skills are required to work effectively in non-church contexts, including the skill of being able to respond in a spiritual way in such contexts and 'putting that kind of theological framework on the basic stuff of life'.

Supermarket chaplain

Kim spends two hours twice a month as a voluntary chaplain to a supermarket in the parish where she is a self-supporting Ordained Local Minister. She felt a personal call to this kind of ministry after hearing a talk called 'Meet on the Street' at a New Wine evangelical Christian gathering. She responded to the supermarket advertisement for a chaplain, applied and was appointed. The local store manager had been told to appoint a chaplain by the company, although he did not know what a chaplain was. As a consequence, Kim has no job description or contract. This means that there is no structural embeddedness in the context, no accountability and no organizational rationale for the role. The appointing manager has since left, leaving the continuance of the role dependent on the relationship with the next manager.

Kim wears her clerical collar in order to signal her distinctive Christian presence and has made herself a badge with 'Chaplain' and her name on it. She feels tensions within the role given the multi-faith context but these are not addressed with the management. Her availability to talk to people is announced every half-hour over the loudspeaker system and she sees the main focus of her role as being available for pastoral conversations. This includes conversations with people who attend her church with whom she does not usually have opportunity to spend quality time because of the number of people who require her attention after a service. Kim sees this as fulfilling a valuable pastoral role in the community, but she expressed a sense of frustration that there is no real engagement with the role by the management.

Kim sees the role as an extension of her church role. 'It's giving time to say, you folks are valuable, we care about you, the Church cares about you . . . an extension really of parish work.' The title 'chaplain' is 'just a name that's been attached to the job' and is not understood to have any specific delineation: 'I just see it as *me* going in there, representative of the Anglican Church, to be there for people to talk to me or not, and if I can help them or listen to them, that's what I see my role is.' It is seen as 'a big part of the mission of the Church, because if the folks won't come to the church building', then church people 'have got to go out to where the folks are'. Kim usually emails the prayer team at her church before she goes into the supermarket, and the congregation and ministry team are aware of what she does. This is experienced by Kim as supportive, along with the conviction that it is where God wants her to be.

YMCA chaplaincy

The YMCA hostel for single people had a Church Army captain as chaplain until two years previously when the local church took on the involvement with a team of about eight volunteers who visit on a rota basis. Peter, the vicar, is officially the chaplain, but he doesn't take a lead role. He sees the work as part of the mission of the Church as 'ministry beyond our walls' and the importance of it as residing in the opportunities it offers to build 'relationships between Christian and non-Christian as the basis for ministry'. The volunteers don't have any particular training or support, because 'they're all pretty experienced Christians'. The main involvement is running a games evening once a week as the basis for building relationships and trust. Occasionally, residents go to church events, and the church is establishing a pioneer congregation, which they hope will establish links with the YMCA. Peter would like to see more links with the Christian faith as a next stage of involvement.

The chaplaincy is seen as being there for the residents only, and there is no substantial engagement with the staff or management. The work is referred to as 'chaplaincy' only within the YMCA, 'because I think that's how they see things', but 'in church it's just seen as part of the work'. Although Peter is nominally chaplain, he says, 'I don't do chaplain things, whatever those might be.' There is no job description for the role, but the fact they are still welcome leads Peter to assume that the YMCA is happy with their involvement. The church has recently appointed a pioneer minister, and he hopes to develop his role in the YMCA by visiting during the day. The church wants to encourage people to attend a pioneer service, 'a kind of Fresh Expression in the pub'. It already has an ecclesiological framework for its thinking in what it calls Discipleship in Action, 'communities based in particular locations around the parish'. Peter's hope is that the work in the YMCA will inform how they go about developing more of these ecclesial communities.

The case study story

The description of this study shows how a town centre team ministry has developed chaplaincy roles as part of an intentional strategy for missional engagement with the community in which it is set. The team rector articulates a theology of mission that underpins the team strategy and an understanding of the role of chaplaincy within that. However, there is clearly a wide variety of chaplaincy practice within the team and the chaplains articulate and enact different understandings of what chaplaincy is and of how it relates to parish roles and to the mission and ministry of the Church.

The Market Town Study: The development of chaplaincy roles within a market town ecumenical project

The context

The context for this study is the creation of an ecumenical project as a missional response to the challenge of changing social and ecclesial realities. In the context of dwindling congregations and diocesan reorganization requiring a reduction in numbers of full-time stipendiary clergy, the churches in the town looked afresh at how they could most effectively communicate the gospel. In the light of the Anglican–Methodist covenant of 2003, the main Anglican churches of the three parishes in the town met with the Methodist Church to discern the way forward. This resulted in the amalgamation of the three parishes into one large parish, and in 2009 a covenant was signed with the Methodist Church in a joint commitment to mission and ministry in the area.

The strategic thinking behind this development was set out in a report for consultation called *How Shall We Sing the Lord's Song in a Strange Land?* (Churches Working Group 2008). In this document, the main missional benefits of shared working are detailed as: churches being able to do more together than on their own; releasing time, energy, talents and resources by pooling human and financial resources; giving church representatives a stronger voice in the community by enabling them to speak on behalf of not one church but many; strengthening the Christian witness by coming together in mission with the Methodist Church with one voice. The missional vision for the churches is that they are called not just to support the faithful few and 'to live in splendid isolation, but to be involved in the midst of this needy world, working alongside and with all people'.

The new structures and governance that this reorganization implies enabled the planning of new shared mission initiatives: a full-time worker with children and young people; a shared administrative post; a part-time chaplain to the further education college; and a part-time chaplain to older people working with residential and nursing homes and with older people in the community. It was envisaged that more chaplaincy roles might develop as the covenant relationship matured, for example chaplaincy to large retail businesses. In this case, it is clear that from the inception of the project, chaplaincy roles have been understood as a key element in the desire of the churches to better serve the mission of God in the world. The study now describes how this vision for the work was realized in practice from the perspectives of key project members.

The vicar

John, one of the main architects of the reorganization, described how the expectation in a small market town that ministers will be involved in most things meant that while they developed a wide variety of skills, they had little opportunity to fully develop one aspect of the work. It was decided that it would be a better use of resources for individuals to concentrate on key areas of church life rather than everybody trying to do everything. This led to the concept of clergy having 'functional responsibilities', such as education and adult discipleship, rather than responsibilities for a particular building and congregations. This required a change in church responsibilities, so that instead of dealing solely with one building, a minister would be responsible for particular congregations, perhaps in different church buildings.

This concept established a principle of specialization which in turn raised the question of limits. For example, a focus on education entailed demands from several primary and secondary schools and a further education college with 2,000-plus students. It was recognized that, given these demands, developing worthwhile work in the college while being a parish minister was 'virtually impossible'; in his own perception, John had done this not very well for four years due to the lack of time. It became apparent that a partnership would be successful only if the minister was sufficiently part of the college structure, so that they were known by and knew the community. This led to the idea for a jointly sponsored chaplaincy role, and it was agreed that for a trial three-year period, the college and the church would co-fund one day a week of term-time chaplaincy. John sees this development as the movement from one minister having responsibility for an area of work to them devolving part of that responsibility to someone who can spend more time in a context. The logic is that 'You cannot effectively do it (the work) sometimes unless you are part of the structure you're trying to work alongside and support.' The same logic is seen as applying to the appointment of the chaplain to older people: 'So the chaplaincy initiatives come out of the first decision that there needed to be functional responsibilities . . . and the location of some of the posts outside of the church structure relates to an assessment of the practicalities of actually doing it.'

The commitment to missional outreach into the community is seen as a driver for chaplaincy initiatives. Chaplaincy is seen as important because it enables the Church to step into key areas of the life of the town where it felt it needed to have more of an input. John identifies the underlying theology as being that 'God is concerned about everybody, and those of us who are called are called to be concerned about everybody'. It is this principle which 'feeds the ecclesiology which then feeds looking for an approach that's going to do that'. The distinctive thing about chaplaincy is that 'you're specializing on one aspect of community life and often in a limited number of geographical locations or types of people'. It brings to the team the ability to raise issues about God's purposes in secular organizations which would otherwise be 'resistant to the casual approach of the parish priest', enabling the Church 'to know enough about our neighbour in order to open meaningful conversation . . . in a way that might improve things'.

However, from the Church's point of view, these initiatives can be problematic, 'because once you set up something outside of the church structure, in a sense you lose partial control of it'. John's experience is that the time pressure on parish clergy means that unless a proactive management approach is taken with specific times set for meeting, it is easy to lose touch with chaplains. Chaplaincy is seen as part of mission, but 'a dangerous part of mission' unless you are in a position to manage it well and to integrate it with the rest of the work, 'and that is difficult'. John is clear that supervision is required in order to reflect on what is being done and how effective it is. Both the chaplains in the project are line-managed by clergy, with the further education chaplain also having a line manager in the college. Questions of accountability relate to questions of funding: although the two main chaplaincy posts are part funded by external bodies, they are also resourced by the churches. This raises for the project the challenging issues of the communication and integration of chaplaincy roles with the wider life of the churches.

John observed that although a lot of effort is put into keeping congregations informed about the work, many people don't take up the information and remain uninformed. This makes it difficult to address issues about the ways in which congregations may perceive chaplains: are they seen as doing the work for them and so alleviating them of any responsibility, or do the chaplains try to link congregations with the work so that they are seen as encouragers of the work? It is difficult to find effective ways of communicating, and John notes that when there is pressure on resources, and congregations are asked what they want, 'they always say clergy'. This means that mission takes second place, and chaplaincy is easy to cut. 'So we need to help the congregation understand what we're doing and buy into it or else they won't fund people who on the face of it aren't doing anything directly for them.' John notes that this applies not only at the local level but also centrally where there is a recent history of chaplaincy posts being cut. Chaplaincy therefore presents many challenges to the churches:

> It challenges them to take mission seriously; it challenges them to think of them working within other people's structures; it challenges them to make the effort to understand what's going on; and it challenges them to fund something that they may not get any direct returns from . . . So it is a challenge to congregations to have that level of vision, to look outward rather than inward . . . and I think that's a big ask really.

The new structures and working practices require active management, and John reflects that clergy who develop such projects need to be properly trained, resourced and supported by bishops who understand the vision. He believes that what is needed is people who can see 'the big view' of what the Church is doing in terms of mission: there needs to be 'a serious engagement with individual communities' and that involves looking at structures and ways of working.

Older people's chaplain

Clare is an Anglican Reader, who is technically employed for 20 hours a week by the Methodist Church and is line-managed by the Methodist minister in the project. The post was part-funded by a charity that provided tapered funding in order to establish the post. There is a significant and growing population of older people in the town, which was identified as a locus of ministerial need during the reorganization process and to which the establishment of this post was a response. Clare is involved with four care homes providing a mixture of nursing, residential and specialist dementia care. She is also in touch with several groups of sheltered accommodation and will see people in their own homes by invitation or appropriate referral. Clare was prompted to apply for the post in the light of her personal experience of having parents in a care home whom she recognized could have benefited from having someone outside the family to talk with about their spiritual needs. She relished the opportunity to forge this role as she wished, and began by establishing good relationships with key people and voluntary groups in the community along with the staff and managers of the care homes. This has provided the foundation on which the work has been built, and Clare sees relationship-building as key to the development of the role with both the care and church communities.

Clare is aware that she works 'very much as a representative of the congregations', and the work is supported by a small group of lay people. Although the chaplaincy role is a specialist role with a clear focus on ministry with one section of the community, Clare sees it also as collaborative, supplementing what the clergy were already doing. She works with the clergy to provide services within the homes and regularly attends relevant parts of team meetings. She preaches at times and has established an annual 'In Celebration of Age' service for the whole community. She is thus involved in the liturgy of the parish. Clare's professional background is journalism, so she is very aware of the importance of good communication and of the need to represent the work to others effectively. She has produced a DVD about her work to explain what is distinctive about this form of chaplaincy and to encourage others to explore their own vocations in this area of ministry. She was keen to develop a small group of lay people to work alongside her and to test their own vocation to the work.

The specialist nature of the role means that she has built up knowledge, networks, relationships, trust and expertise in the area in a way that parish clergy do not have time to do. This includes locating appropriate training for herself given that there is no specified training. She believes the fact that she does not have the bureaucratic and administrative workload of a parish minister 'frees me to go where I identify the needs'. Although she does have the structure of key services that she takes, and there are certain administrative tasks and records to keep, 'what's distinctive about being a chaplain is that I can respond to needs very quickly'. This freedom to encounter and respond to people in the midst of daily life is deemed by her to be precious and distinctive of chaplaincy.

Clare understands the role as being for everyone, whether or not they espouse a religious faith. In her view, being a lay person also means that she is less likely to be perceived as being potentially judgemental:

> The beauty is that I can come and meet people exactly where they are, and I seek to be completely non-judgemental. And if a conversation never mentions God, that's fine, it's about ministering to the total person wherever they may be on their spiritual journey.

She may be 'Church' for some people who have lost touch with their churchgoing history, and for others 'just a friendly face', but her self-understanding is that she is being sent by the congregation and that 'Christ goes before me and that I'm there to embody that sense of love and trust'. Clare sees this as very much part of the mission of the Church at a time when there is 'so much despair and lack of hope'. She reflects that the Church forgets the important priority which she sees as 'to remind people that they are loved by God and that they are cared for and cared about by their Creator and by other people from the cradle to the grave and beyond'.

In the care homes, Clare regards herself as being there for the whole institution, residents, carers and staff, as well as having a representative role within the wider community as a point of contact to talk about issues relevant to old age. Part of her remit is to be an advocate for older people, and she perceives the need to develop a role concerning how people prepare for their own older age. She believes that anyone in this role needs to be an empathic listener and to have the capacity to give full attention, focusing on the other's 'whole wellbeing'. This means that the chaplain needs to have thought through his or her own spirituality and to have worked through the losses in his or her own life. Dealing repeatedly with loss and sadness highlights the importance of good support and supervision, ensuring that appropriate boundaries are kept and that time for replenishment is taken. Clare thought that chaplaincy work requires different personality traits from parish clergy, 'Someone who has that individual drive and personality . . . to resource their own work . . . you've got no one necessarily cracking a whip.'

Clare ended her interview by saying that she felt that being a chaplain was something to be proud of and that it was 'fine work'. She was shocked to realize that not everyone in the Church appreciated the work, especially individuals who had power over the allocation of resources.

Methodist minister and line manager of older people's chaplain

Like John his Anglican colleague, Tom locates the rationale for the development of chaplaincy roles as both missional and pragmatic. Just as the Anglican diocese reorganized, so the Methodist

Church was 'regrouping for mission' posing the same question of how to best serve the local community. It seemed obvious that the best way for the churches to bear witness to the gospel in the town would be to work together: 'We felt that . . . God's Spirit was involved very much in what was happening . . . and that we were involved in something which was bigger than us as individuals, bigger than us as individual churches . . . it was about how could we best minister, mission and serve the community so it wasn't just church based, it went beyond that.' This focus *ad extra* was the impetus for the developments: whatever reorganization took place, it needed to serve that end. The willingness of churches and individuals to 'grasp the bigger picture' made change possible at a particular time which Tom sees as 'God's time': people recognized that there was something of God in what was being proposed. Tom now thinks that chaplaincy is a major contribution that the project makes to the town and surrounding areas and that people take the churches more seriously because there is a bigger dynamic than one church acting alone.

From outside the Church, this may give the work more weight and authority than one church might have had, but within the churches the case for the missional focus of the chaplaincy work has had to be made. A perception that chaplaincy diverts resources from the Church into the community has had to be addressed. Tom sees that the older people's chaplain has done this effectively by her involvement in both church life and the community. Clare is known and seen both by people in the care homes and at church events, so that church people understand her work. People appreciate the role and are prepared to support it, because they have had a positive experience of it, and 'it's because the experience has been so positive, it would be far easier to sell . . . another brand of chaplaincy to people who have already seen that it works'.

This raises the question of how to quantify what is 'successful'. As Tom says, there are no tick-boxes for being the person who enables someone to voice their innermost fears. However, he suggests that one could look at signs of a chaplain functioning well. This might include good working relationships between the chaplain and her or his context, positive feedback and the work that is accomplished. A further criterion would be that the organization in which the chaplain works values the work and, if possible, is prepared to contribute resources. In care homes, benefits might be seen in terms of lower staff turnover, and a chaplain might be able to contribute at management level, bringing questions about good practice and staff support. 'So you can bring gospel, kingdom ethics to that.'

Tom sees the distinctive identity of chaplains as residing in their ability to invest time and energy in a context in a way that general ministry no longer allows. Chaplains are representative ministers who become specialists in their field and are able 'to feed that back into the life of the churches and the project and the community'. He draws the analogy of chaplains as specialists to whom the parish priest as GP would refer someone. However, chaplaincy is not just about skills and opportunity, 'There's something about calling: not everybody can be a chaplain.' Tom identifies a difference between how you relate to people as a chaplain and as a Methodist minister. For him, this relates to the capacity to be available and approachable to people, to listen and to work in an open and non-judgemental way engaging with people where they are. As a chaplain, 'You've got to be the kind of person who's not hiding behind . . . the formal title or the dog collar, or the role or the liturgy or the paraphernalia that ministry often brings.' In a culture where many have no connection with a faith community, it's about helping people to find a language in which they can articulate their deepest human experiences and 'accepting people for who they are and not for who you want them to become. It's about being the yeast and leaven: it's kingdom stuff.' Ultimately for Tom, 'It's about being Christ's presence in the world . . . it's about being with the people who are broken, neglected, on the edges . . . marginalized, misunderstood: it's about being where people are . . . It's not about being within the structures of what the Church has to offer.'

Tom sees chaplaincy as central to the mission of the Church, because 'It's bringing God and God's kingdom and God's word and values into wherever people are.' The development of chaplaincy posts inevitably brings challenges to the churches, because it asks, 'How big is your vision of the Kingdom? How big is your vision of what God is doing? Is God only at work in the life of the Church or is God at work in the life of the world?' He acknowledges that chaplains may also bring unforeseen challenges to the Church through feedback about pastoral practice with particular groups such as older people. However, a good working relationship between chaplain and church which enables positive feedback to be given and received can facilitate learning and enrich the faith community.

Further education college chaplain

Annie works one day a week during term-time in a post jointly funded by the college and the churches. She is a former teacher and a part-time curate in the parish. The college has about 2,000 students and 200 staff. Her line manager in college is the lead counsellor in Student Services, and she is supervised in the parish by the associate vicar. The church developed this role as a proactive engagement with the college, and the college sees it as an important dimension of their equality and diversity agenda. There is a small number of Muslim and Buddhist students, a variety of Christian denominations and the majority who say they're 'not anything'. Both the college and Annie see it as a multi-faith role in that 'It is an embracing role of those of all faiths and none . . . So I suppose it's more of a general spirituality, nurturing role encouraging youngsters to explore.' Annie wears a clerical collar as a 'badge of office', but she also has a bright orange hoodie with 'College Chaplain' on it. She is transparent about who she is as a person of faith but is happy to engage with anyone.

Annie sees her ministry in college as being underpinned by 'the gospel imperative of caring for folk as Christ did – unconditionally'. She encourages people of different faiths to explore their own beliefs and values and is aware that some in the church would find that difficult. However, she says 'I'm firm in my faith', and she believes that sharing her faith enables people to consider where they are. Her view is that if the 'fundamentals of Creation' and the love of God are the same in every tradition, 'Who am I to judge, to say, "Actually, believe in this way"? I can't do that. I think God is bigger than all of it.' Annie acknowledges that her outgoing personality suits the context and the role which is 'what I make it really' in contrast to her more prescriptive curate's role. The college has resourced her with a room, used by the counsellors in her absence, but which she has been able to make her own and which provides a base where interested students know where to find her. However, the foundation of the work has been going out and about, engaging with students and staff by 'tapping in to where they are', building a profile for chaplaincy and building relationships. Her approach is to set up activities that students want to do and that come from them, and a lot of time is spent networking and getting involved in the life of the community. For example, she had taught a lesson with the Buddhist A-level group and supported staff through a time of cuts and redundancies. Her priority is to 'engage' and 'to capture the imagination of youngsters to think'.

Annie sees the work as 'an embracing mission' in that:

by my example and my care and my outreach, I hope to live my Christian faith and to stand firm in that Christian faith while not making judgement on other folk who come from a different direction . . . So I don't feel compromised in the slightest because I feel that that Christian outlook, sharing the love of God, is the whole purpose of chaplaincy.

Associate vicar and supervisor of further education college chaplain

Mark is responsible for education and discipleship across the parish and supervises Annie. Because the further education chaplaincy is located within an institution, he describes it as being 'self-contained', suggesting that 'it could go on almost entirely divorced from the life of the parish', unlike the chaplaincy to older people which is more integrated. He perceives that the danger inherent in there being little interaction 'between the established churches based on a parochial model and the chaplaincy that they're supporting' is that the chaplaincy brings little to the project apart from relieving people of some responsibilities and that it is hard to foster a sense of it being owned by the parish and the Methodist Church.

This sense of ownership and integration with the parish work is seen by Mark as vital if the churches are going to support the work financially. People, he says, will inevitably ask, 'What do we get for our money?', but there are also the important questions, 'Why are we doing this?', 'What does this really mean?' and 'Can we relate to this in something more than theory?' For Mark, this ministry needs to be understood in the context of the vision of the whole project, and he is not certain that this has yet been clearly enough articulated. He suggests that they need to look at how the chaplains can be 'more present in more of the communities of the church' and at how they represent their work and achievements to people. This may be a difficult symbiosis to achieve given that 'I think the chaplains have a much clearer idea about what they think they're doing than the rest of the parish.' This is another of the challenges that the chaplaincies pose to the project, along with challenges about 'how we see particular groups of people'. He is not sanguine, reflecting that the parish is probably 'not in a good position to even see the challenges'. The 'gap' between chaplaincy and parish ministry is seen by Mark as partly a function of everyone being over-busy, so that there is no time to reflect together on the work: an intentional process of integration requires time and space. Ultimately, Mark locates this challenge within the wider ecclesial context of change:

> I think there's a long way to go in integrating this model with day-to-day parish ministry and that's going to be compounded by the fact that the nature of parish ministry is changing and the nature of the institution of the Church is changing and may not be able to survive very long anyway.

Mark sees the distinctiveness of chaplains as residing in the fact that they are appointed to a role because of the particular gifts and skills that they bring to an area of ministry, and they are then given the time and authorization to focus on that area. The basic value to the whole Church is that ministry is done that would otherwise not be done and that the Church is present in places that it would otherwise not be: chaplaincy is 'really good PR'. Chaplains are part of the mission of the Church, particularly in secular institutions like the college:

> To have a chaplain there who can encourage young people to address what it means to be human and what it means to relate to others and what that means about the value of life and the value of other people is very important. And it is about mission in that it is about promoting the possibility of a Christian view of the world.

For Mark, the emphasis lies on the value of the contribution that chaplaincy can make to human flourishing and the common good:

> The value to *humanity* is more important than the value to the Church . . . I'm not sure that it matters whether it's valuable to the project or not, it's whether it's good for the institution concerned and good for the young people concerned . . . and the fact that we're able to facilitate that, *that's* the important thing.

The case study story

This study describes how structural reorganization and pressure on human resources in the Church was grasped as an opportunity to rethink parochial structures and ways of working in order to enhance the effectiveness of mission and ministry in one area. Through a consultation process, ecumenical working was established as central to the theological, missional and ecclesial thinking that was undertaken, and a vision and strategy for the churches' work produced. Within this vision, chaplaincy was positioned as strategically important to the missional engagement with the community that the churches wanted to achieve. However, the actual practice of chaplaincy brought to light tensions between ways of working, different perceptions of chaplaincy and priorities for ministry. It also presented the difficult challenge of finding ways to explain and integrate the vision for chaplaincy within the context of the Church and parish focus.

Conclusion

These stories provide evidence of the relationship in practice of theologies of mission, be they operant (implicit in practice) or consciously espoused[1] and the development of chaplaincy roles in specific community contexts. Subsequent chapters draw on this evidence as the discussion of the three main themes developed from the data and their representation in these stories provides the basis for developing a theological and ministerial rationale for chaplaincy within the mission and ministry of the whole Church. At a time when human and financial resources are limited, chaplains are ever conscious of the need to demonstrate the value of their work in the context of the Church's default prioritization of the parochial model of ministry. If the significance and value of chaplaincy within the mission of the Church is to be understood, the theologies of mission that underpinned and shaped the development of these chaplaincy roles need to be described and placed within the wider, normative missional narrative of the contemporary Church. It is to this task that the next chapter turns.

---

1 The Four Voices of Theology model describing operant, espoused, normative and formal theological voices is presented in Cameron et al. 2010.

3

Chaplaincy Within the Mission
of the Contemporary Church

Introduction

One of the most significant findings from the case studies described in Chapter 2 was that all the participants identified chaplaincy work as central to the mission of the contemporary Church. The studies revealed a pervasive awareness that the Church needs to find ways of connecting with the majority of people who no longer relate to a faith community and that chaplaincy roles represent a significant way in which the cultural gap between churchgoers and non-churchgoers might be bridged. In order to understand more fully why this might be the case, it is necessary to consider some of the challenges that the contemporary cultural context offers the mission of the Church before discussing the part the theologies of mission evidenced in the case studies played in the emergence of chaplaincy roles in response to that wider cultural context. This discussion will enable individual theologies of mission to be brought into relationship with the normative missional theology of the wider Church. It is hoped that the locating of chaplaincy within the mission of the Church may provide a context within which the voice of chaplaincy has more chance of being represented and heard than has hitherto been the case.

The contemporary cultural challenge to the mission of the Church

Several research participants echoed the observation of the supermarket chaplain in the Town Centre Study that if people won't come to the church building, church people need to go out to where people are. This points to the central challenge to the Church of finding ways to reconfigure itself in order to connect with the majority of people who are closed to institutional belonging but open to 'God' and the transcendent. Finding ways to do this has been one of the central concerns of the churches over the past two decades, as they have sought to engage with the consumer-led, fluid and dispersed character of contemporary, post-Christendom life in which belonging to an institutional Church is a minority choice. This remains the challenge of a changing culture to the churches.

As noted previously, the Church of England report *Mission-Shaped Church* (Archbishops' Council 2004) recognized the challenge that contemporary culture had set the Church. The development of Fresh Expressions, 'emerging church' and the training of Pioneer Ministers were all responses to this basic need to find ways of connecting with people the traditional Church was finding it increasingly hard to reach. The report quotes a much older World Council of Churches report (WCC 1968, cited in Archbishops' Council 2004) in order to characterize the nature of the contemporary missionary task:

> The missionary task remains the same: 'A changing culture constitutes a call from God. Many people today live in a variety of worlds such as family, job, leisure, politics and education. These worlds represent different social structures.' The gospel must be proclaimed afresh within these different structures. (Archbishops' Council 2004, p. 13)

The report goes on to suggest that the perceived decline of the Church may be ultimately caused 'neither by the irrelevance of Jesus, nor by the indifference of the community, but by the Church's failure to respond fast enough to an evolving culture, to a changing spiritual climate, and to the promptings of the Holy Spirit' (p. 14).

The Church is still faced with the challenge to pay attention and respond to the three contextual dimensions identified in 1968: an evolving culture, a changing spiritual climate and the promptings of the Holy Spirit. With reference to the first of these, the evidence suggests that the recent growth in chaplaincy roles represents one way in which the Church is responding to a rapidly evolving culture characterized by constant movement and change. It has been argued that geographical location has declined in significance as networks virtual and otherwise have become the characteristic locus of social interaction and people constantly move between social structures. As Ballard (2009) has noted, in this cultural context the chaplaincy model can be seen as an attempt to express the relevance of the gospel to every area of life, each requiring a particular response.

The significance of chaplaincy as a response of faith communities to this evolving cultural milieu is reflected in media interest in chaplaincy such as the commissioning of the BBC2 series *Chaplains: Angels of Mersey – Taking Faith Out onto the Streets with Liverpool's Chaplains* (BBC 2012) and the more recent *Children's Hospital: The Chaplains* (BBC 2014). The 2012 series offered a collage of diverse models of the engagement of representatives of different faith communities in a variety of contexts under the umbrella term 'chaplaincy'. This umbrella use of the term for any kind of faith-based engagement with society is common. It raises the question that will be addressed in the next chapter of what the term actually means. For the moment, it is telling to note how chaplaincy was characterized in the commentary: 'Chaplains are modern-day disciples . . . they take the word of God out of the church and into the places we work and play.' This popular conception of chaplaincy echoes nicely, if unwittingly, the research findings that suggest that the development of chaplaincy is a direct response, consciously or unconsciously, to this missional challenge to the churches. It also implicitly contains the two other main themes developed from the research: the question of what 'chaplaincy' actually is and the ecclesial question of what the Church is and the relationship of chaplaincy ministry with church ministry.

The second dimension identified in the 2004 report as requiring an ecclesial response is 'the changing spiritual climate'. The rise to prominence of 'spirituality' was identified in Chapter 1 as one of the significant cultural currents relevant to the growth in chaplaincy. Davie was perceptive enough to observe in 1994 that 'Religious life . . . is not so much disappearing as mutating, for the sacred undoubtedly persists and will continue to do so, but in forms that may be very different from those which have gone before' (Davie 1994, p. 198). This view was borne out by the more recent research of Heelas & Woodhead (2005) with their conclusion that traditional forms of religious association are giving way to and being influenced by new forms of spirituality for which engagement with personal experience is a key component. Their thesis was that underlying the contemporary turn from religion to spirituality is the 'subjectivization' of culture within which the self-authenticating authority of personal experience takes precedence over demands to conform to external obligations.

This cultural phenomenon has been linked to religious traditions (Tacey 2004) with the suggestion that if they are to continue to thrive, they need to pay heed to personal experience and to recognize it as a potential locus of revelation. This intimation is picked up in the research in the way in which, for example, the town centre chaplain and the chaplain to the homeless charity cite Jesus' ministry as the model for their chaplaincy work: just as Jesus ministered in the community, revealing the sacred in the midst of the experience of everyday life, fishing, tax gathering, drawing water, sharing food, so the Church needs to focus on revealing the presence of God in the everyday structures and experiences of people's lives. Davie (1994, p. 200) suggests that many parish churches find it increasingly hard to connect with this cultural milieu, 'for they continue to provide . . . a production rather than a consumption version of religion; providing, that is, a consistent pattern of worship and pastoral care, dictated by the obligations of their role'. It is this difference of emphasis that is picked up in the studies by, for example, the agricultural, older person's and further education chaplains. Across the diverse contexts, all of them remarked on the contrast in their experience between the entrepreneurial, responsive approach of chaplaincy and the more prescriptive role of parish ministry. The studies suggest that chaplaincy, characteristically located within social rather than ecclesial structures, provides ways and means for the Church to come alongside people in the midst of daily life, to engage with those who have little or no connection with the Church and to address individual and social concerns by listening to individual and social experiences and being ready to respond appropriately.

It is this open and dialogic approach to missional engagement that is characteristic of chaplaincy as presented in these studies. It is this approach that enables the discernment of and response to the third dimension identified in the 2004 report, namely the promptings of the Holy Spirit. The Methodist Minister in the Market Town Study recognized the promptings of the Holy Spirit as underlying the impetus for change and ministerial reorganization. In a way that is directly relevant to the discussion of chaplaincy, Pickard (2009) discusses the need to attend to pneumatology in his exposition of an ecclesiology of ministry that could serve the mission of the Church today. In Pickard's view, writing as an Anglican, in order for there to be a truly collaborative ministry that can focus its energies on mission, attention needs to be paid to the relationship between a christological and a pneumatological approach to ministry. An overemphasis on christological representation can lead to a static ontology of orders and the prioritization of clerical over lay ministry and of ministry over the Church. Set alongside this is an understanding of ministry as that of the whole Church, the theological foundation of which can be located in 'a renewed emphasis on the work of Christ through the agency of the Spirit' (2009, p. 17). This recovery of the dynamic relation between christology and pneumatology is seen by Pickard as the theological promise central to recent developments in the understanding and practice of ministry. This approach prioritizes charisma over institution and characterizes ministry as 'an emergent *charism*-generated activity of the whole Church. The community of faith, under the guidance and inspiration of the Holy Spirit, receives and exercises the gifts of God for the common good, witness and service: the mission of the Church' (2009, p. 36).

In the light of this understanding, chaplaincy may be seen not only as responsive to the work of the Holy Spirit in the world, but the growth in roles may also be seen as a response to the Spirit's promptings within the Church. This view may have particular relevance given the number of lay people involved in chaplaincy ministry. With the recent development of different types of ministry in response to the cultural challenges facing the Church, the importance of an ecclesiology of ministry which can help to make sense of the relationships between ministries is clear. One of the main themes developed from the research is the relationship between chaplaincy and parish ministry; until attention is paid to this relationship, the false, disempowering and dis-spiriting dichotomy between 'chaplaincy' and 'the Church' that is so prevalent is likely to be perpetuated.

I have described some of the contours of the cultural context with which the Church is seeking to engage. Awareness of this context and the challenges it presents is key to the way participants in the studies thought about mission and the role that thinking had in the development of chaplaincy roles. It is now necessary to look more closely at the theologies of mission that underpinned the development of chaplaincy roles in order to be able to place these understandings in the context of a wider contemporary understanding of the Church's mission.

Theologies of mission in the case studies

An operant theology of mission

In the Rural Benefice Study, Chris, the agricultural chaplain, is embedded within both the church and the farming community. Most of the people she works with as a chaplain don't attend church, but the strong relational basis of trust that she has forged within the farming community provides the basis for her chaplaincy work. The role enables her to engage with farmers where they live and associate, to listen to their individual and social concerns, to respond flexibly to those concerns and to take their experience seriously as the starting point for that engagement. Although she is a distinctive Christian presence, she is aware that it is who she is in that role that really counts with the community; they trust her because they know that having been a farmer, she will understand their concerns. She recognizes the reciprocity at the heart of her involvement with a community that she cares about deeply when she remarks: 'Now I don't farm anymore, it's given me an excuse . . . to go into the farming community and still be part of it.'

The role has not been developed intentionally as part of a mission strategy for engaging with and serving this community because Chris was already engaged with it as a farmer herself. However, she does see the role as missional in that it is located in the structures of rural life and enables her to work across parish boundaries in order to engage with people who would otherwise have little or no contact with the Church. Although Chris understands chaplaincy work as missional, she is clear that it is not about getting people to come to church but about 'bringing God into people's lives at a time when they are vulnerable without ramming it down their throats'. It is about being available as a representative Christian person to listen to people's lives and experience and to what they need to say in order to be able to discern where God's Spirit may be at work in the world and to co-operate with the Holy Spirit in ways that contribute to human and social flourishing and thereby to the establishment of the Kingdom of God.

Chris is aware that great sensitivity is needed in this task. In order to build good communication and trust, it is often necessary to work in what Morisy (2004) terms the 'foundational domain', enabling people to engage with the intimations they may have of an enduring reality, rather than in the 'explicit domain' of gathered church life and the language of traditional Christian symbolism. While the explicit language of faith may often not be evident,

Chris is aware that in what she does, what she offers in the service of the community and in who she is for the community, she is collaborating with God's mission in the world. As she says, 'I'm doing all this with God.'

In this case, the theological dimension of the work characteristically remains implicit in the practice and through the distinctive presence of the chaplain who has been formed in the faith tradition. There is a commitment to the nurturing of people's faith, the opening of spaces of grace where healing and hope can flourish and to possibilities for transformation on a personal or systemic level. This operant theology of mission, incarnated in practice, understands service and pastoral care as being core dimensions of the Church's vocation to serve God's mission in the world. It accords with Hull's (2006, p. 2) assertion in his critique of *Mission-Shaped Church* that the Church is not the fulfilment or flowering of mission: 'The flowering of mission is the Kingdom.' However, in the Rural Benefice Study, this theology is not explicitly articulated and consciously espoused, so that it can be represented to others as part of a rationale for the work.

The mission of the Church and the missio Dei

The other case studies evidence much more explicit thinking about the relationship between theologies of mission and the development of chaplaincy roles. This thinking about practice has been undertaken in the context of developments in understandings of the Church's mission over the last 20 years in relation to the concept of the *missio Dei*. According to Heywood (2011, p. 1), over that period 'Mission has moved from the periphery of the Church to its centre.' It is no longer seen as an optional activity undertaken by a particular kind of church, but rather the Church's core identity is understood as being constituted as the bearer of God's mission in the world. This missionary calling derives from an understanding of the very nature of God as missionary. The community that Jesus gathered around himself was to be a visible sign that the Kingdom of God was arriving in him. In the Gospel of John, Jesus entrusts the mission of God to this community, saying: 'As the Father has sent me, so I send you' (John 20.21, NRSV).

Theologies of mission grounded in the concept of the *missio Dei*, such as the seminal work of Bosch (1992), highlight the nature of the Church as 'sent' into the world to establish the Kingdom in the particular circumstances of everyday life. This is mission understood as 'the good news of God's love, incarnated in the witness of a community, for the sake of the world' (1992, p. 519). As Heywood remarks, 'Rather than following a universally applicable blueprint, the community is called to discern the shape of God's mission for each place and time and to allow its own life constantly to be renewed by the Holy Spirit so as to fulfil that mission' (p. 113). I suggest that this is precisely what chaplaincy ministry seeks to do.

The Rural Benefice Study illustrates the deep missional instinct at the heart of the establishment of the chaplaincy role. Chris understands that if that missional discernment is to take place, the Church needs to be alongside people, listening, paying attention to where the Holy Spirit may be at work in the world. The heart of the approach is relational and this has a deep resonance with the understanding of mission in Western theology as grounded in the participative relationship of the Trinitarian life of God. Spencer (2007), for example, presents mission as the outpouring of this relational life into the world, inviting and drawing others to share in its life-giving exchange. This approach understands the heart of mission as relational, because God is relational, and if mission is grounded in participative relationship, it cannot be one-way but must always be marked by genuine dialogue and mutual exchange. Such contemporary understandings of mission rest on several underlying theological principles: the importance of the Kingdom of God understood as God's reign over and involvement with the whole of Creation; the importance of the work of the Holy Spirit in Creation; and the consequent understanding of Church as called into existence for the sake of the whole of Creation.

In accord with this understanding, Spencer (2007) presents a paradigm for mission that addresses the contemporary context

characterized as 'finding hope in local communities'. This is particularly helpful in thinking about chaplaincy ministry and the
nature of ecclesial involvement in community contexts. Spencer
endorses the common theme he finds in the work of Bonhoeffer
and the cross-cultural missionary strategy with the Masai presented in Donovan's *Christianity Rediscovered* (1978), that of 'the
Church laying aside its power and wealth and becoming vulnerable to the local community, listening before witnessing, changing
and being changed by the encounter'. This paradigm suggests that
in a plural, multi-faith context, it is in the willingness to engage in
genuine dialogue that opportunities for authentic witness occur.
In the context of local communities, it is in the offering of service
and the giving and receiving of hospitality and care that opportunities arise. The important components of mission in the contemporary context are thus identified as: listening before witnessing,
humility, encounter, mutuality, reciprocity, dialogue and depth
of discipleship. A similar perception led Bosch (1992, p. 375) to
suggest that we need to speak of the Church 'with' and alongside
others rather than 'for' others as part of 'God's identification with
the world in the sending of the Son'.

This contemporary emphasis on reciprocity and relationship
being at the heart of mission echoes Taylor's contemplative exposition of mission in *The Go-Between God: The Holy Spirit and
the Christian Mission* (1984). Dated as this may now be, it
issued an important call to the churches to pay attention to
the work of the Holy Spirit in the world, in the 'extraordinary
ordinariness' of people's daily lives. This call is still valid and it
may be that chaplaincy is in a position to take up the call afresh.
Taylor suggested that if mission is understood as participation
in the life of God in the world, then 'the heart of mission is
communion with God in the midst of the world's life' (p. 227).
In this view, the fundamental missionary activity is to live in
prayer characterized as a permanent attentiveness to Christ's
indwelling presence or, in St Paul's words, to 'Pray in the Spirit at
all times' (Ephesians 6.18), so that the whole of our lives bear witness to our faith, lived out of that deep communion. In the words
of Jenny, the community missioner in the Town Centre Study,

this is about 'setting up mission as life, not something we do on occasion'.

Taylor's core belief that our relationship with our neighbour mirrors our relationship with God reflects the influence of the Jewish philosopher and theologian Martin Buber, whom Taylor studied and who has been influential in my own thinking and practice of chaplaincy. In *I and Thou,* Buber (1958, p. 32) states that 'the relation with man is the real simile of the relation with God'. In Buber's work, the life of the Spirit is manifested between persons who enter into relationship with their whole being; relationality is therefore fundamental to living the life of the Spirit. This suggests a sacramental understanding of the world as the arena of God's activity, and of genuine relationships as holding the potential to be a place of encounter, revelation and transformation. This stream of thought, harnessed by Taylor, provides further theological underpinning of the concept of the *missio Dei*. It spotlights the significance of the relational dimension of mission that is central to the study of chaplaincy with its location within social structures and its focus on pastoral care and service. It suggests that 'it is the quality of and approach to relationships that holds the potential to bear witness to faith and to be revelatory of God's presence at the heart of Creation' (Slater 2011).

In the Rural Benefice Study, there is no worked-out espoused theology of mission cited as a reference point for the development of the role, but the case nevertheless demonstrates the deep missional impulse at the heart of the process. Chris understands that the vocation of the Church is to be 'sent' into the world to be alongside people in relationship. She understands that it is the relational foundations of trust that enable people to talk about the reality of their experience and that this is the starting point for discerning what God might be doing in people's lives and how the chaplain, as representative of the Church, might best serve that mission. This is mission understood as co-creative collaboration with God's work in the world; it seeks to collaborate both with God and with the communities and people it serves. The emphasis on relationship as core to chaplaincy work places it directly within the above understanding of mission as a gracious overflowing of the relational life of God, characterized by Spencer (2007) as the outpouring of the Trinitarian dance-like life of mutual participation into the world. It invites others to share in this life-giving way that is marked by a mutual giving and receiving recognized by Chris in the sense of community that the work gives to her and which calls for certain qualities and ways of working in those who embrace this kind of theology of mission.

The development of chaplaincy roles within espoused theologies of mission

In contrast to Chris's story, Paul, the team rector in the Town Centre Study, articulates clearly the relationship that he sees between a theology of mission and the development of chaplaincy roles within the team. He has used the *Mission-Shaped Church* report (Archbishops' Council 2004) as 'a framework to work from' in thinking about mission. It was an imperative that the Church should engage missionally with the town and its people, and chaplaincy was seen as a prime mode of engaging in this context. The town centre chaplain points to the churches' deepening awareness of the cultural gap between those who attend church and those who do not and the need to find ways, such as chaplaincy, through which the Church can bridge that gap. The widening of this cultural gap may have given pragmatic impetus to the missional imperative, but if such initiatives are to be effective and sustainable, they need to be underpinned by a theology of mission that can locate them within the wider strategic narratives of mission within the Church. It is this theological connectivity that could enable those within church structures to understand the rationale for chaplaincy posts and, in understanding, perhaps be more prepared to support and resource them.

Paul talks about the underlying theology of mission in terms of 'sentness', a missional sense that he felt needed enhancing in the town centre church. This awareness of the need for the Church to go out to engage with people where they are is conceptualized in terms of the need to move from a fairly passive role for the Church in its social context to a more active one. He describes this as a move from a dominant Benedictine mode of engagement based on hospitality to develop a complementary peripatetic Franciscan mode alongside. The development of chaplaincy has played a central part in this intentional shift in emphasis. Paul reflects that this shift has impacted on congregations in the way that they now see their ministry and the involvement that they have with the local community through the various chaplaincy and community initiatives.

This points to the reciprocity at the heart of chaplaincy and missional engagement as described above. The process of the development of chaplaincy roles with the enhanced opportunities for church members to offer themselves in service to the local community has enriched the life of the church and vice versa, thus enacting Spencer's paradigm of mission as 'finding hope in local communities' (Spencer 2007, p. 175). It requires the Church to lay aside any privilege or power that it may have and to become vulnerable to the local community in a commitment to authentic engagement and dialogue. If it is to be effective, this approach needs to be undertaken with humility and a recognition that both parties in the dialogue may be changed by the encounter. Listening to people in their context and genuine dialogue are essential modes of effective chaplaincy engagement with today's cultural context. As Percy (2006) notes, most ecclesial communities are having to react and evolve with the environments in which they are set rather than shaping them from some position of inherited privilege. This research suggests that chaplaincy offers a positive contextual model of ministry that meets this contemporary cultural challenge. Within today's plural, multi-faith context, dialogue and witness need to enter into dialectic, for it is often in genuine encounter and dialogue that the opportunity occurs for authentic witness. This witness is expressed through Christians offering themselves in service to local communities so that, according to Spencer, 'they may give and receive hospitality and care and so that genuine dialogue and witness may take place' (Spencer 2007, p. 180).

Morisy (2009, p. 110) echoes Bosch's suggestion (1992, p. 375) that we need to speak of the Church 'with' rather than 'for' others in her contention that the Church and its representatives need to understand themselves not as achieving some kind of 'success' in relation to community involvement but as *being* a contribution to the flourishing of the whole. This returns to an emphasis on relationship and collaboration with others rather than the rewards of status and power that come with 'success'. As she points out, the rewards that come from being a contributor are 'deep, enduring and hopeful'. Heywood endorses this approach, suggesting that when this is the case, the chaplain is not there to uphold the Church's institutional presence but 'as a sign of the social, moral and even spiritual significance' of the life of a particular community (Heywood 2011, p. 14). What is then chiefly valued about that person's presence is not what sets them apart, but what brings them alongside, 'a shared humanity, vulnerability, a willingness to share the struggle, to explore the meaning of the mundane activities through which social life is maintained, perhaps to offer the hope of a better world'.

This missional paradigm is exemplified in Chris's ministry in the Rural Benefice Study and accords with Jenny's description of the intention behind the development of her role as community missioner and police chaplain in the Town Centre Study. The aim was to establish a distinctive Christian ministry in the town centre, being available to listen and to engage in genuine dialogue with people on a social network basis beyond the traditional boundaries of church life. She begins from the premise that God is already present and active in the world, and so the Church needs to be 'getting out there'. Kate (town centre), Jenny and Peter (homeless charity), all cite Jesus' ministry, going out to encounter people in the midst of their everyday lives, as the model for chaplaincy, and Jenny suggests that the Church needs to learn this afresh. What bears witness to those outside church structures is the quality of authentic discipleship, which is why abuse of power, discriminatory practices and acrimonious internal debates are antithetical to that witness which in Jenny's words is about 'setting up mission as life, not just something we do on occasion . . . when are we going to learn that every little thing we say speaks for God?'

The dialogic and collaborative approach to mission demonstrated in the studies exemplifies in practice Volf's characterization of the relation between Church and culture, based on the exegesis of the New Testament first letter of Peter, as 'soft difference' (Volf 1994, p. 7). Volf addresses the question of how the Christian community lives out its identity in a particular cultural context, suggesting that soft difference, as opposed to a harsh approach, is 'the missionary side of following in the footsteps of the crucified Messiah' and that it is part of Christian identity itself. 'To be a Christian', he says, 'means to live one's own identity in the face of others in such a way that one joins inseparably the belief in the truth of one's own convictions with a respect for the convictions of others'. It is this kind of approach, for example, that is articulated by Annie in the Market Town Study, when she states, 'I hope to live my Christian faith and to stand firm in that Christian faith while not making judgement on other folk who come from a different direction' (Further Education).

There are, of course, different perspectives on chaplaincy and its relationship to a theology of mission within the variety of practice represented in the Town Centre Study. This is evident, for example, in the involvement with the YMCA and the supermarket where the work is seen as an extension of parish ministry rather than as having a ministerial identity in its own right. This raises the question of the identity and integrity of chaplaincy as a genre of ministry that will be discussed in the next chapter. However, what can be said of this study is that the theology of mission espoused and described by the team rector was instrumental in the strategic development of chaplaincy initiatives as a means for the Church to fulfil its calling to participate in the *missio Dei* for the flourishing of the Kingdom and as part of the sending of God.

The pragmatic need for the Church to find appropriate forms of mission and ministry to enable it to engage with people it is finding it hard to reach is certainly one factor behind the explicitly stated strategic missional thinking that underpinned the establishment of the ecumenical project in the Market Town Study. As in all the studies, the challenge to the churches was how to offer Christian witness and service to the majority of the population who do not engage with a faith community. In the description of this case in Chapter 2, I described how added impetus was given to the imperative to find ways of engaging with the local community by a diocesan reorganization that required a reduction in the number of full-time stipendiary clergy. The response to this changing social and ecclesial context was to collaborate with the Methodist Church in a process of theological and strategic thinking in order to establish structures and models of working that could enable the churches to be as effective as possible in serving the community of which they were a part. The development of chaplaincy roles in this context occurred therefore within an explicitly described espoused theology of mission and an ecclesiological model of working, both of which were set out in an initial consultation document (Churches Working Group 2008). This document provided a theological and strategic framework for thinking about mission and service beyond the gathered congregations, but crucially it also set out the structural and governance framework that the implementation of such a vision would require.

Although tensions between chaplaincy and church-based ministries are evident in each case study, it is in the Market Town Study that the importance of the relationship between missiology and ecclesiology comes to the fore and is explicitly addressed. The consultation document recognized that if scarce resources are to be used effectively to serve God's mission, then ecclesial structures need to be put in place that will enable that to happen; new models of working needed to be developed if new initiatives were to grow. The strategic model of functional specialization that was developed, described in Chapter 2, released human and other resources for the development of shared mission initiatives including specialist chaplaincy roles. Given the constraints on ministers' time and, according to John the vicar, the reluctance of congregations to engage missionally, chaplaincy was seen as an important strategic means of church engagement in the community. According to John, what is needed in terms of the Church's mission is 'a serious engagement with individual communities'.

All three case studies emphasize the participatory and relational foundation to chaplaincy ministry in accord with the grounding of mission within an understanding of the participative relationship that is the Trinitarian life of God. Grounded in this life that constantly flows into the world, chaplains seek to collaborate with the perpetual creativity of the Holy Spirit. This collaborative, relational understanding of mission refers back to Taylor's (1984, p. 147) call to the churches to pay attention to the work of the Holy Spirit in the minute particularities of everyday life. Taylor reminded people that 'the Church is essentially scattered, like seed in the earth, salt in the stew, yeast in the dough. The Christian's milieu is the world because that is the milieu of the Holy Spirit.' There may have been theological, strategic and pragmatic motivations for the development of chaplaincy in the Market Town Study, but Tom, the Methodist minister, pointed out that in the coming together of so many dynamics in a particular time and place, people felt that the Spirit was at work and that their human efforts to understand how to participate in God's mission were part of a larger picture, that this was 'God's time' too. The development of new structures and roles was understood as the Church responding to the promptings of the Holy Spirit, part of the threefold responsiveness to the changing cultural context identified as necessary to the Church in the *Mission-Shaped Church* report (Archbishops' Council 2004) quoted above.

In the Market Town Study, the fact that chaplains work on different models from parish ministers and that they are located significantly within non-church structures raised challenges for the churches and questions about the relationship between the different genres of ministry that were also coming to the fore in the Town Centre Study. As John remarked, chaplaincy challenges the gathered Church to take mission seriously and therefore 'to fund something that they may not get any direct returns from'. This *is* serious. Just as missional initiatives in the Town Centre Study challenged the town centre congregation to develop its own missional identity, so here the missional dynamic of chaplaincy flows towards the Church as well as the community. John reflected that at a time of limited resources, if congregations are asked what they want, 'they always say clergy; they want some-one to look after them, which means that mission . . . takes second place'. If they are to rise to that challenge, they need to be helped to understand chaplaincy as an integral part of the mission of the Church, 'or else', as John says, 'they won't fund people who on the face of it aren't doing anything directly for them'. This implies that even those who uphold the parish system can be captured by a consumption model of religion within which they are reluctant to resource anything that does not give them a tangible return on their investment. This is the difficult challenge posed by the development of chaplaincy roles in ministerial contexts.

Conclusion

This chapter has considered the ways in which operant and espoused theologies of mission in the case studies have shaped the more or less strategic development of chaplaincy roles. It has presented the development of these roles as a Spirit-led ecclesial response to a changing culture. Chaplaincy is here characterized as a response to the perennial missionary task, set out in the *Mission-Shaped Church* report, to proclaim the gospel afresh in the contemporary context. In this plural, fragmented and largely de-churched society, this means that chaplains are called to minister within the different social structures that people inhabit.

If a changing culture does indeed constitute a call from God, then rather than the development of chaplaincy being viewed as random and marginal to the central missional concerns of the Church, this development can be seen as an ecclesial phenomenon that is central to those concerns. In the Town Centre Study and the Market Town Study, the development of chaplaincy roles was seen as a central component of the Church's strategy for mission: in the words of the Declaration of Assent made by all authorized ministers in the Church of England, it is part of the Church's historic commitment to bring 'the grace and truth of Christ to this generation' (Archbishops' Council 2000, p. xi). Chaplaincy has been located within the *missio Dei* theology that has become central to contemporary understandings of the Church's mission and within a relational and collaborative paradigm of mission that prioritizes finding hope in local communities. Positioned thus, chaplaincy can be seen to be a significant contribution to human and social flourishing and thus to the building up of the Kingdom of God. It is also revealed as central to the mission of the contemporary Church and, as such, requires serious theological reflection and the allocation of appropriate resources.

The evidence suggests that implicit or explicit theologies of mission have a key part to play in the development of chaplaincy initiatives, but also that once roles are established, tensions between chaplaincy and church structures of ministry often come into play. Are chaplains just re-located parish ministers or do they have a particular vocation and identity? If they do, what characterizes that identity and how does it relate to the institutional Church? These are questions that the parallel phenomena of Fresh Expressions and Pioneer Ministry have wrestled with and which have led Goodhew, Roberts & Volland (2012, p. 19) to locate them within the apostolic tradition of the Church. However, a considerable amount of theological reflection has been resourced by the Church in relation to Fresh Expressions and Pioneer Ministry while the historic ministry of chaplaincy has been left on its own to develop. The fresh significance of chaplaincy for the contemporary Church has, as it were, crept up on the institution unawares, and there has been little rigorous reflection on practice. Having established the missional importance of chaplaincy, it is therefore the above questions that the next two chapters need to address.

4

What Makes Chaplaincy 'Chaplaincy'? The Identity and Integrity of Chaplaincy as a Genre of Ministry

Introduction

The evidence presented and discussed in the previous two chapters shows that theologies of mission play a key part in the emergence of chaplaincy roles. It also shows that once roles are established, tensions between chaplaincy and church structures of ministry often come into play. A good example of this is the part-time town centre chaplaincy in the Town Centre Study. The studies show that congregations and ministerial colleagues may not understand the value of chaplaincy ministry and may therefore be reluctant to support the work. Before such tensions can be addressed, it is necessary to understand what makes chaplaincy 'chaplaincy': if people do not understand what the term actually denotes, it is not surprising that they cannot see its value within the mission and ministry of the Church. This chapter therefore begins by looking at the problem of understanding what 'chaplaincy' means and what the nature of chaplaincy might be. It asks some fundamental questions which are often not considered when people talk about chaplaincy: What are we talking about? Does chaplaincy have a particular identity and integrity? If it does, what characterizes that identity and how does that relate to parish ministry and the institutional Church? In answering these questions, I will suggest three core dimensions that are characteristic of chaplaincy roles even though their contextual responsiveness means that they may look different in different contexts. These dimensions delineate the identity and integrity of chaplaincy within the Church's ecology of mission.

I have referred to chaplaincy throughout as a *genre* of ministry, as this is a term particularly apt to the task in hand. The Cambridge online English dictionary defines 'genre' as 'a style, especially in the arts, that involves a particular set of characteristics'. In relation to chaplaincy ministry, it suggests the contextual responsiveness of chaplaincy which does involve 'a particular set of characteristics' that can be identified, but one which may be expressed differently as the context requires.

The problem of 'chaplaincy'

The fundamental difficulty that besets discussions about contemporary chaplaincy is the lack of conceptual clarity about what it actually is: people tend to talk about chaplaincy on the assumption that everyone knows what they are talking about. However, it is almost as slippery a word as 'spirituality'. It is therefore necessary to describe an understanding of the concept in order to bring coherence to the discussion. Traditional understandings of chaplaincy as referring to Christian clergy 'commissioned by a faith group or an organization to provide pastoral service in an institution, organization, or governmental entity' (Swinton 2002, p. 1) have changed in response to the challenges of the contemporary plural context. There are now lay and volunteer chaplains, chaplains of different faiths, Humanist and inter-faith chaplains, and Christian chaplains will typically find themselves working as part of a multi-faith and/or ecumenical team. It should also be noted that some practitioners would not want to be called 'chaplain' either because of its Christian origins or because of its perceived connotations in cultures such as healthcare where the remit has broadened from a primary focus on religious care to a focus on more generic spiritual care. Todd notes that in multi-faith contexts, using words such as 'ministry' to define chaplaincy can be problematic because it comes from a particular faith tradition.

He therefore chooses to use the more neutral term 'practice' and defines chaplaincy as 'a practice exercised by faith practitioners, on behalf of faith communities, but dispersed within other communities, institutions and organizations' (Todd 2007, p. 6). This definition currently locates most, though not all, chaplains, but it does not address the issue of understanding what it means to be called a chaplain and what the parameters might be for a practice to be chaplaincy.

This is particularly the case in community contexts where many roles emerge in an ad hoc way. In institutional contexts such as hospitals and prisons, most chaplains do at least have a job description and contract with the organization within which they work: there is some consensus about the identity of the role. This may not be the case in community contexts as seen in the Rural Benefice Study and the supermarket chaplain in the Town Centre Study. This state of affairs is worrying on many levels, not least in relation to ethical questions of competence and accountability. Conceptual clarity about the role requires competence and accountability. This is essential given that chaplains often work with vulnerable people. With so many people now developing chaplaincy-type roles, it is currently a focus of scrutiny for both the churches and the academy. *The* question that they have to ask into this complex situation is: 'What is the identity and integrity of chaplaincy?' In other words: what do chaplains do, what do they think they are doing and how do they do it?

Although the focus here is on Christian chaplaincy, even in this context the studies suggest that there is no common understanding of what it means to be a chaplain. Cobb (2004, p. 10) puts the issue succinctly in relation to healthcare chaplains when he asks: 'What is it about being a chaplain that causes them to define themselves as similar to one another; and what is it that causes others to recognize or attribute common characteristics in them by which they can be categorized as chaplains?' Until a convincing response to this question can be given, the use of the term will lack clarity and integrity. Furthermore, until the identity of chaplaincy and the particular set of characteristics that being a chaplain involves can be described, it is hard to see how the crucial issues of selection, training, resourcing and the development of faithful practice can be addressed. It is also difficult to see on what basis conversations with parish ministers located within church structures and conversations with the institutional Church can take place.

With this question of identity in mind, I will now draw on the research evidence to suggest three dimensions of chaplaincy that need to be reflected on in relation to practice if effective chaplaincy roles are to be established and sustained. Although not all chaplaincy roles will exhibit all the characteristics described within these dimensions, they do provide some basic parameters within which chaplaincy can be recognized as chaplaincy and best practice can be developed and sustained. This could also enable chaplaincy to be represented coherently to others be that in a secular context or the Church. It is important to say that this is not a model of chaplaincy. The construction of a model could have tended to solidify findings into an ideal representation and might well have struggled to accommodate the diversity of practice. Rather, I have chosen to adopt a more descriptive approach that is able to be congruent with the findings while remaining open and able to function as a catalyst for further thought and development.

Interpretations of chaplaincy in the case studies: what is chaplaincy?

The different perceptions of chaplaincy found in the studies focus the problem of talking about it as a genre of ministry: there is little or no conceptual clarity. It is clear from the studies that chaplaincy not only looks different in different contexts, but that it is understood and perceived differently depending on the theological, ecclesial and vocational standpoint from which a person views this ministry.[1] At one end of the spectrum, chaplaincy can be used as a 'flag of convenience' under which ministry can be

---

1 I use 'ministry' to describe chaplaincy in the studies, because all the participants were authorized Christian ministers and all the roles had emerged from ministerial contexts.

undertaken in a community context. Thus in the Town Centre Study, Kim, the supermarket chaplain, remarks: 'It's just a name that's been attached to the job', while Peter, the YMCA chaplain, sees it as an extension of parish ministry, explaining that 'we don't refer to it as chaplaincy within our church. We refer to it as chaplaincy within the YMCA, because I think that's how they see things . . . in church it's just seen as part of the work.'

It is clear from this that being an authorized minister does not offer any conceptual clarity about what it means to be a chaplain. Neither Kim nor Peter had a role description or contract with the respective organizations and both were volunteers. The organizations had not specified what they expected a chaplain to do, and the supermarket had no concept of what a chaplain was. Kim and Peter perceived chaplaincy to be part of their church-based work and the designation 'chaplain' simply as enabling them to be present as church representatives in a secular context. This implies that their ministerial identity remained entirely rooted in their ecclesial context rather than being in dialogue with the social context of their chaplaincy. At the other end of the spectrum to this pragmatic use of the term, some participants perceived chaplaincy to be a vocation in its own right. For example, Kate, the town centre chaplain, explained that even at the time of her selection for ministerial training, she knew that she didn't want to be a parish priest. 'I wanted to be a chaplain.' People like Kate and Clare in the Market Town Study express a deep vocational commitment to working outside church structures and alongside people in the midst of their daily lives. Although Kate is also a parish priest, her ministerial identity is shaped by her chaplaincy experience. She is convinced of the value and identity of chaplaincy as a genre of ministry in its own right and has thought about the characteristics that constitute its identity.

The dimensions of chaplaincy

Such divergent perceptions of what it means to be a chaplain simultaneously epitomize the difficulty of saying anything at all about it and the necessity to do so. Given that chaplains work in the public square, they are in effect practical apologists for the Christian faith, the place where people in the secular world meet the Church. It is therefore important that they are able to give an account of their practice: what they do, what they think they are doing, and the skills, knowledge and gifts required to do it. This is necessary not only for the development of faithful and effective chaplaincy practice but also to enable a mature and creative dialogue to take place between those working within church structures and those working as chaplains within social structures for the sake of those they seek to serve. Furthermore, if a narrative of chaplaincy that can be interpreted both to secular organizations and to the Church can be constructed, it is more likely that it will be able to elicit the resources it needs. After all, organizations, including the Church, will only resource work they understand and value as contributing to the mission of their organization. The importance of this is suggested, for example, in the further education chaplaincy in the Market Town Study, where its contribution to human flourishing and the common good are understood by the organization as contributing to its equality and diversity agenda. The following three dimensions provide a framework for such a narrative.

Theological integrity: chaplains are called and sent

The previous chapter discussed the ways in which particular theologies of mission formed the basis of strategic thinking about chaplaincy development in the studies. This missional theology was echoed by the majority of the participants, as in Kate's reflection that:

> for me, chaplaincy is being out there with people, wherever they are, and I think that's the difference to being in a church . . . you're sent out . . . , but I think it's more than that, I think it's actually showing the compassion of Christ . . . in a way that is not always seen in a church setting. (Town centre chaplain)

The first characteristic therefore is that chaplaincy is missional in its commitment to serving the mission of God in the world. In order to be able to fulfil this calling to listen and discern how and where God may be at work in the world so that an appropriate response can be made, this ministry needs to be substantially located in the structures of society. In the Market Town Study, John described this dynamic in relation to the creation of the further education college chaplaincy post:

> We realized that really it would only be successful if the person from the church working in the college was sufficiently part of the structure for everybody to know them and for them to know what was going on. (Vicar)

This is a theological and ecclesiological imperative which understands the vocation of the Church as being sent into the world, walking alongside people in their need and daily living, contributing to the flourishing of the Kingdom of God as part of God's sending (Bosch 1992). As Clare reflected:

> It's about ministering to the total person wherever they may be on their spiritual journey . . . And then I personally am going feeling that I'm being sent by the congregation but that Christ goes before me and that I'm there to embody that sense of love and trust. (Older people's chaplain)

This leads to the conclusion that the primary ministry of the chaplain is not to build up the existing empirical Church or to establish Fresh Expressions of Church, but to embody and express God's love and grace with and for those who gather in a particular institution, place or network, to express the values of the Kingdom of God and to witness as appropriate to the Christian gospel. This is the incarnational heart of chaplaincy.

In offering this ministry, chaplains fulfil in an intentional and representative way the discipleship to which all Christians are called in order to contribute to human and social flourishing. In ecclesiological terms, chaplains therefore can be understood as the dispersed Church, intentionally fulfilling its vocation as the community of people called and sent to serve and witness in the world. As Goodhew, Roberts & Volland (2012, p. 104) assert in relation to Fresh Expressions, 'Church is church whenever and wherever people gather around the risen Jesus – it is also Church when scattered as salt and light in the everyday contexts of work, leisure and personal relationships.' However, as I will discuss in the next chapter and as Brown (2011, p. 4) notes, what may be the distinctive vocation of chaplaincy may also locate the gap in understanding between chaplaincy and church structures as being not about differing interpretations of the gospel but about 'the priority which should be given to maintaining and building up the empirical church of the here and now'.

Chaplains go to where people are, working collaboratively within other people's structures and in critical solidarity with those who gather in a particular context, whether or not they profess a particular faith. This 'guest' theology, discussed in Chapter 1, was articulated by Kate: 'In the retail park . . . it is not a place as the role of the chaplain to evangelize because . . . we are a guest on their ground. We have been invited in by the management team' (town centre chaplain). At the heart of any chaplaincy role is a nuanced relationship with the particular context. There is often a strong empathy with the context in which a chaplain works with the sense of calling stemming from the chaplain's own experience. For example, Clare's experience of her own elderly parents needing spiritual support led to her involvement in older people's chaplaincy. Perceiving a need and the opportunity for involvement, the impetus is to serve the community with which they have empathy and understanding in order to contribute to its flourishing and in so doing to bear witness to God's involvement with every dimension of human life just as the Incarnation, the sending of the Son, bore witness: 'God in Christ reaches out to human beings wherever they are. He comes to us. He does not wait for us to come to him' (Goodhew, Roberts & Volland 2012, p. 37).

There is a strong perception within the studies that the fundamental model for chaplaincy is Jesus' ministry, that chaplains are a continuing part of that sending. For example, in the Town

Centre Study, Paul reflected on chaplaincy as 'a visible sense' of the Church's presence in society, saying, 'We're an incarnate church, so God just didn't give us the idea of incarnation, he actually sent his Son to demonstrate it, and in a sense, that's what chaplaincy is living out' (team rector). Likewise for Stuart, Jesus' ministry is cited as the model for chaplaincy, being 'outside meeting people . . . where they were and when the opportunity arose to talk with them about spiritual things' (homeless charity).

The research evidence therefore suggests that the theological integrity of chaplaincy can be found in its missional, incarnational and dominical character which focuses on the service of the *missio Dei*, the building up of the Kingdom of God and contributing to human and social flourishing. Chaplains go to where people are, rather than waiting for people to come to the Church, providing 'a very clear presence beyond the church's walls' (team rector), a ministry in the public square. This means that chaplains are in a position to be practical theologians in public life, working out theology amidst the daily particularities of life. This missional focus is underpinned by an ecclesiology that is dispersed, collaborative, ecumenical and actively involved with the whole of life. The chaplaincy practice in all the studies revealed a strong underlying theology of mission in which the chaplains' self-understanding and their understanding of the Church they represented had at its heart a clear sense of being called and sent to be in the world in order to collaborate with God's mission. This theological, ecclesial and social location of chaplaincy has particular implications for the ministerial identity of chaplains, the second dimension to be considered.

Ministerial identity: a distinctive, representative and recognized presence

Before considering what constitutes the ministerial identity of chaplains it is necessary to clarify what is meant in this context by the term 'ministry', given that it is used to denote both the service that is common to all Christians and particular differentiated forms of service within the Christian community. It is used here to refer to a form of Christian witness and service that is representative of the Christian community in a way that is publicly acknowledged and accountable. In a similar vein, the Methodist Church (2012) has noted that the difference between being a Christian witness and being a chaplain is that 'a chaplain is essentially recognized by the host organization'. While this is not wholly constitutive of chaplaincy identity, it is an essential parameter for chaplaincy that has fundamental implications for the ways in which roles are negotiated, set up, resourced and sustained, as well as for how chaplains understand their own identity.

A good example of this is the further education role in the Market Town Study which was negotiated between the church and the college and was jointly funded. The role was recognized by both communities such that Annie was line-managed within the college and supervised in a church context. She had a contract, job description and office space. She was clear about her own faith commitment and the representative nature of her role but also that she was available to everyone, whether or not they had a particular faith commitment. This was to ensure that, as far as possible, people across the organization received the pastoral and spiritual care that they needed. Participation in and understanding of the context enabled Annie to engage in a particular structure of relationships as a chaplain that had been unavailable to the parish priest, who had previously only had the capacity to visit occasionally and was not part of the everyday life and structures of the organization.

This intentional participation in critical solidarity with a context establishes ministerial focus and relationships beyond the gathered faith community and thereby builds a particular ministerial identity. Chaplains, to a greater or lesser extent, are embedded in a particular social context, seeking to understand that context from within while still maintaining their identity as representatives of a faith community and their capacity for prophetic witness alongside pastoral care and service. This is a complex place and identity to inhabit: not everyone is called to exercise this genre of public ministry and not everyone has the skills or capacity to do so. Cobb (2004) suggests that the meaning of being a chaplain is realized in relationship to others and therefore chaplaincy identity is 'intrinsically social'. In accord with this insight, the case studies revealed the multivalent identity of chaplains and the negotiated nature of that identity. As Cobb reflects, 'Chaplains cannot simply go around claiming a particular identity; the communities they relate to and deal with must validate it.' In contrast to parish ministry in which one could argue that an explicit faith identity is primary, in chaplaincy where relationships are often primarily with people who have no explicit connection with a faith community, what is required is a nuanced and sophisticated capacity to negotiate one's identity in response to particular circumstances. Chaplains constantly participate in several different cultures and communities which may include the chaplaincy context, society, their faith community and often chaplaincy itself. This means that they need to understand the discourse and culture of each, to be, metaphorically, at least 'tri-lingual' (Todd 2007) and skilled at cultural interpretation. This requires a mature faith identity and a high degree of cultural and self-awareness.

For example, in the Rural Benefice Study, Chris is constantly aware of when it is and is not appropriate to use explicit faith language. She is aware that witness is often made as much by who she is, her presence, the nature of her relationships and what she offers the community, as by any specific religious discourse that she may use. Although she is an authorized minister, her identity and authority to minister within the farming community are validated by the community itself. 'It's because they know me as a farmer that they will talk, they know that I would understand.' Formed and rooted in her faith tradition, Chris is able to meet people where they are without imposing an agenda upon them. This capacity is referred to explicitly by Annie in the Market Town Study, when she describes her inclusive ministry of encouraging people to explore their own faith and values saying: 'But I'm firm in my faith, I know where I stand, and I think that is how to get people to consider where they are.'

The evidence suggests that where people have been able to establish their identity as a chaplain, an identity validated and accounted by the context within which they serve, then chaplaincy is able to make and be an effective and valued contribution to the common good based on relational trust, mutual respect and understanding. This in turn enables chaplains to challenge practices as well as to offer support. As Jenny says in the Town Centre Study, 'It's about being a critical friend; being in the midst of a place where you are welcome, but you also have an opportunity to challenge expressed views and practices' (police chaplain). The evidence also suggests that where the role is not understood or validated by the organization or network, as in the instance of the supermarket chaplain, then it is extremely difficult, if not impossible, to establish an identity as a chaplain and therefore to develop an effective and sustainable chaplaincy practice.

The evidence also suggests that when people feel confident and validated in their identity as a chaplain, they are able to be themselves in their role. This means that they are able to come alongside people in order to listen to their experience and to share, when appropriate, the recognition of a common humanity and vulnerability. Both the town centre chaplain and the chaplain to the homeless charity refer to the fact that, as a chaplain, the key point is who one is in the role. Kate reflects that 'it's very much your personality that's out there. They have their expectations but expectations of you perhaps as a person and not as a priest or chaplain' (town centre chaplain). Tom in the Market Town Study put this starkly. He was clear that at times chaplains need to be willing to share themselves in genuine dialogue and conversation: 'You've got to be the kind of person who's not hiding behind . . . the formal title or the dog collar or the role or the liturgy or the paraphernalia that ministry often brings' (Methodist minister).

What then can be said to characterize the ministerial identity of chaplains? The evidence discussed above suggests three primary marks of chaplaincy:

1 Chaplains fulfil a representative role that focuses the vocation of the Church to serve the mission of God in the world.
2 The chaplain's role is publicly recognized and validated.
3 Chaplains are appropriately accountable to the host organization or network as well as to their faith community.

The main characteristics comprise:

- A focus on serving the *missio Dei* in the world rather than on the internal concerns of the institutional Church.
- Being rooted and formed in the faith tradition.
- A focus on meeting people where they are, both socially and personally.
- Having an empathy and understanding of the context with which they stand in critical solidarity.
- Being open to construct an effective chaplaincy identity in dialogue with the social context within which they are embedded.
- The capacity to be culturally 'multi-lingual' in order to offer and witness to the insights and values of the faith tradition in a culturally plural context in ways which contribute to human flourishing and the common good and so to the flourishing of the Kingdom of God.

This profile suggests that the ministerial identity of chaplains is theologically grounded but contextually shaped as the chaplain collaborates with the social context within which she or he works to offer a contextually responsive ministry of service, critical pastoral care and prophetic witness. As presented in Chapter 1 (Fig. 1), chaplaincy, at its best, is essentially dialogic, constantly in dialogue with different cultures and discourses including those of the Church. It is rooted in a deep commitment to human flourishing. It pays attention to people's lived experience, understanding it as a potential locus of revelation, and it flourishes on the capacity to build relationships of mutual trust and respect. This ministerial orientation is captured in Mark's reflection on the value of the further education chaplaincy in the Market Town Study: 'In a sense, the value to the Church is that that's really good PR . . . but in a sense, the value to *humanity* [participant's emphasis] is more important than the value to the Church' (associate vicar). To adapt Davie's (1994) categories of production and consumption versions of religion, chaplaincy arguably offers a consumption version of ministry that can, at best, respond with imagination, creativity, flexibility and integrity to the challenges and opportunities it encounters in a plural society.

Consideration now needs to be given to the qualities and skills needed by chaplains to establish an appropriate and effective identity and practice. This is the third dimension: professional integrity.

Professional integrity: skilled and responsive to challenges and opportunities

Chaplains characteristically work collaboratively with different professional groups and within other people's structures. They also work with vulnerable people such as the instances of elderly, young and homeless people in the case studies. If they are to build relationships of trust and mutual respect within their working context, it is important that they work in a safe and professional way that ensures they have appropriate knowledge and skills and that they are accountable and resourced. At present in this country, the question of the professionalization of chaplaincy in the community is not on the agenda. This would entail development along the lines of established professions in order to achieve recognized professional status. What is relevant and needs to be addressed is the question of what it means for chaplains to offer a public ministry in a professional way. The diversity of practice and understandings of what it means to be a chaplain described in the studies highlights the importance of detailing elements of the professionalism that is an essential dimension of basic good chaplaincy practice.

At one end of the spectrum, the designated chaplaincy role in the YMCA had no role description. There was no negotiated understanding with the organization as to what chaplaincy might be, and it was seen by those from the church who undertook it as falling within the collective term of 'church work'. At the other end of the spectrum, the town centre, further education and older people's chaplaincies suggest what the elements of an appropriate professionalism might include. The elements can be described with reference to the older people's chaplaincy in the Market Town Study as it demonstrates the main components.

Elements of professional chaplaincy practice

Ethical integrity

Unlike healthcare chaplaincy, for which the UK Board of Healthcare Chaplains has produced a Code of Conduct to which registered members subscribe, there is no code of conduct for chaplains working in community contexts. However, Clare had ensured that she was informed about the ethical issues and boundaries relevant to her work with vulnerable adults.[2] This included the important issue of confidentiality. Chaplains need to ensure that they work in an ethical way.

Knowledge and skills

Clare built on her experience and intuitive understanding of the pastoral and spiritual needs of older people and their carers through reading and training as well as reflecting with others on the nature of her chaplaincy role. This enabled her to create a relevant body of specialist knowledge and skills relevant to work with older people and people living with dementia. Chaplains need to develop the knowledge and skills relevant to work in their context.

The ability to be self-directing

Clare recognized this as a key attribute of chaplains. Chaplains need the entrepreneurial ability to recognize and respond to need, to seize opportunities for engagement and to develop the work

---

2 The Church of England's policy for safeguarding adults, *Promoting a Safe Church*, can be found at www.churchofengland.org.

in imaginative ways. Chaplains need to be proactive and able to work on their own initiative.

Accountability

Clare kept a log of her activity and was clear about how she was accountable both in the church and in the community context. Because she was clear about her identity as a chaplain and about the nature and purpose of the role, she was able to represent and communicate what she was doing to others in both contexts. This enabled her to give an account of her practice, which in turn meant that it could be understood, valued and ultimately resourced. Chaplains need to be accountable in their practice.

Support

Support goes hand in hand with accountability: if no one knows what is being done, it is difficult to find or provide appropriate support. Clare was aware of the spiritually and emotionally demanding nature of the work and therefore of the need for ongoing support. She established a small support group comprising people from the parish and met regularly for supervision with her line manager. Chaplains need appropriate support.

Resources

Clare was able to identify the spiritual, emotional and physical resources that were needed to support the work. She accessed relevant training when she recognized a need to learn more about a particular aspect of the work and attended conferences and events in order to share knowledge and practice with other practitioners. Chaplains need to be resourced.

Although these elements of professional practice will be developed and expressed in different ways according to context and the basis on which a chaplain works, the evidence suggests that where they are present, the chaplain is able to develop an effective ministerial presence and identity. They provide some basic parameters within which a chaplain can work safely and with professional integrity and a framework that can guide the development of chaplaincy roles. These parameters are particularly important in emergent roles where chaplains can have a significant amount of freedom to be self-directing and to develop the work creatively in response to immediate challenges and opportunities. The studies suggest that in chaplaincy, it is the elements of professionalism outlined above that provide the symbiosis between structure and freedom that is fundamental to all creative endeavours. It is the theological and professional integrity of chaplaincy that provides the structure which allows the responsive, proactive entrepreneurial approach which participants in all three case studies cherished as a creative and essential dimension of their roles and which has been suggested as a significant dimension of chaplaincy practice (Hayler 2011).

An entrepreneur can be defined as someone who creates and innovates in response to perceived opportunities in order to build something of recognized value. Recognizing that some people may dislike the use of the term with its individualistic and market connotations, nevertheless it does capture something of the responsive and proactive nature of chaplaincy as it works collaboratively to build something of recognized value in a particular context. The important point to note is that chaplaincy is not just about responsiveness but about a theologically and professionally informed and skilled responsiveness designed to build something of recognized value. Chris describes her role in terms of this kind of approach when she says, 'It's constantly evolving depending on what the current circumstances and problems are, and it's distinctive in that it's led by what's going on' (agricultural chaplain). This relates directly to the theological and ecclesial dynamics of chaplaincy which insist on listening to and meeting people where they are in order to be able to make an appropriate response. Todd (2011, p. 13) explicitly identifies this as an 'entrepreneurial theology' implying an openness to identify and seize opportunities offered by God, however surprising or 'secular' they appear to be. It also relates to the understanding of chaplaincy as a calling and the fact that not everybody is able or suited to working in this way. As Clare reflects, chaplains need 'that individual drive and personality to . . . resource their own work, you know to get up and say right, how am I going to tackle today, what do I want to do?' (older people's chaplain).

In addition to the individual qualities and skills that a chaplain may require, these studies also suggest that the capacity to develop an effective professional practice relates to the wider ecclesial structures within which the practice is set: ministry and Church are bound together. One example is the Market Town Study in which chaplaincy roles are developed within the ecclesial context of an ecumenical project that has articulated its understanding of the place of chaplaincy within its structures and within its strategy for mission. In this instance, chaplaincy is identified as a specialist ministry with its own professional identity implying the need to acquire the appropriate knowledge and skills required for ministry in a specific context. John sees it as 'specializing on one aspect of community life and often in a limited number of geographical locations or types of people' (vicar), while Tom makes a direct analogy with healthcare: 'If it was in some kind of healthcare system . . . she'd [the chaplain] be the specialist who the GP would refer someone to. So the Methodist ministers and the parish priests if you like are the GPs' (Methodist minister). This identification of chaplaincy as a specialist role implies a level of knowledge and commitment to a specific context for which the parish minister does not usually have the capacity, because it entails 'doing the research, reading, attending seminars, networking, contact with all the people who are at the cutting edge of what's happening, to become, if you like, an expert in that field, to feed that back into the life of the churches and the project and the community' (Methodist minister).

This understanding of chaplaincy draws on a secular model from healthcare in order to depict an ideal interdependent relationship between chaplaincy and parish ministry. In so doing it acknowledges the particular knowledge and skills required by chaplains embedded in social contexts but omits any reference to the tensions which may be inherent in the relationship. In the next chapter, attention is paid to these tensions.

Conclusion

This chapter has offered an answer to the vexed question of what makes chaplaincy 'chaplaincy'. I have drawn on evidence from the case studies in order to describe three core dimensions that are characteristic of chaplaincy roles and which, I suggest, constitute the identity and integrity of chaplaincy as a genre of ministry:

- Its theological integrity is rooted in a theology of mission within which chaplains understand their vocation as a continuing part of the sending of God into the world in order to serve God's mission and so to contribute to human flourishing and to the flourishing of the Kingdom.
- Its ministerial identity is as a distinctive, representative and recognized ministry that focuses in an intentional way the call to discipleship of the Christian community.
- Its professional integrity enables it to establish relationships of trust and mutual respect within a context and, equipped with the appropriate knowledge and skills, to respond creatively and faithfully to the challenges and opportunities that context presents as part of the Church's ecology of mission.

Of course, it is still the case that the dimensions that I have suggested may be interpreted in different ways and the contextual responsiveness of this ministry means that chaplaincy may look very different in different contexts.

As the research shows, it is clearly the case that not all roles designated as chaplaincy pay explicit or implicit attention to these parameters. However, I suggest that these three core dimensions provide parameters within which best practice can be developed and sustained. They can also provide the basis of a narrative for chaplaincy that can be interpreted in both social and ecclesial contexts. The articulation of dimensions of chaplaincy brings some conceptual clarity to the use of the term and in so doing raises the underlying question of how this genre of ministry relates to church-based parish ministry and to the institutional Church. The characteristic outward-facing nature of chaplaincy also focuses this question. Not surprisingly, this is the third main theme identified from the empirical research. Chapter 5 will therefore look at the relationship between ministry and Church and the implications this has for the understanding and practice of chaplaincy.

5

The Challenges of Chaplaincy: The Relationship Between Chaplaincy and Church-Based Ministry

Introduction

I have been involved with the practice, teaching and research of chaplaincy in different forms since 1989. Throughout my involvement, I have noted the consistent presence of the theme of chaplaincy's disconnection from the central preoccupations of the 'Church' that has already been discussed. This sense of dislocation came out strongly in: a scoping study of chaplaincy that I undertook in 2009; the conferences for chaplains that I have subsequently organized; the collaborative chaplaincy research undertaken for the Church of England (Todd, Slater & Dunlop 2014); and it is represented in this case study research. This perception and experience is echoed by the quantitative data gathered for the Church of England research which revealed that the central Church had no accurate statistics of the number or type of chaplains working on its behalf and that this is replicated at diocesan level. At a consultation for participants in the above research project, although the discussion was nuanced, there was a distinct theme of disconnection in relation to 'the Church' at the local, diocesan and central levels. Although there is a good relationship with chaplains in some dioceses, in others this disconnection is starkly manifested in chaplaincy resources or even chaplaincies being cut.

In an edition of *Crucible: The Christian Journal of Social Ethics* devoted to chaplaincy, Malcolm Brown (2011), writing as Director of Mission and Public Affairs for the Church of England, notes that the literature of chaplaincy has usually been structured around a taxonomy of institutions, while considerations of it as a mode of ministry and mission 'with shared foundations in theology and missiology and common practical challenges' (p. 6) have tended to be neglected. He goes on to affirm the conclusion of a consultation on chaplaincy held at St George's Windsor in 2010 that 'chaplaincy is less about ministry to discrete structures than about the Church's engagement with society and the public sphere in all its fullness' (2011, p. 6). His editorial stance was therefore to commission articles that took a thematic approach to addressing issues relating to chaplaincy rather than articles describing chaplaincy in different contexts. This marked a significant advance in the approach to thinking about chaplaincy and signalled a recognition by the institutional Church of its current limited knowledge and understanding of the contemporary phenomenon of chaplaincy. It is therefore not surprising that a theme of lack of understanding of chaplaincy ministry by the institutional Church is constant in chaplaincy inquiry. This is often voiced in terms of local relationships but is, I suggest, related to fundamental understandings about theologies of mission, about ministry and about the nature and purpose of the Church.

Chapter 3 suggested that the characteristic missiological impulse of chaplaincy is the quest to participate in the *missio Dei*. Chapter 4 suggested some parameters for this genre of ministry which could enable people to see what chaplaincy might look like if it is to be effective in pursuit of this quest undertaken in the public square. Throughout these discussions the question of how chaplaincy relates to parish ministry and to the mission and ministry of the Church as a whole has repeatedly come to the fore as integral to people's understanding and practice of chaplaincy. This suggests that the tensions that exist between the two genres of ministry, noted for example by Brown (2011) and Threlfall-Holmes & Newitt (2011b), point to the fact that ministry and understandings of the Church are interdependent. As Boff (1977, p. 26) noted long ago, 'The problem of ministries is linked to the model of Church on which it is predicated.' Discussion about the relationship between ministries has to go hand in hand with attention to ecclesiology.

The case studies enable us to see in people's experience how understandings of Church inform the relationship between chaplaincy and parish ministry. The fact that the studies are of chaplaincy roles that emerged within parochial contexts means that the participants had to think explicitly about this relationship. This chapter therefore begins by looking at the relational dynamics that emerged within people's experience, before considering these findings in relation to an ecclesiology of ministry which suggests how chaplaincy could be understood in relation to other ministries and in relation to the mission and ministry of the Church as a whole.

Living the relationship between chaplaincy and parish ministry

All the chaplains in the case studies participated in the structures of parochial ministry alongside their chaplaincy roles. This obliged them to pay attention to the relationship between the ministries in terms of personal relationships, theology and understandings of the Church. Understandings of this relationship have practical implications when scarcity of resources and organizational issues compel people to reflect on how to work together effectively in a changing cultural and ecclesial context as exemplified in the Market Town Study.

In the Rural Benefice Study, the need to attend to this relationship is not felt acutely, because the chaplain works on her own and is embedded in the farming and rural communities in both her chaplaincy and parochial roles. In practice, the relationship is construed as a personal issue of time management. She is supported in managing the roles by the churchwardens and together they are clear that the parish work takes priority. Even though

Chris is deeply committed to the chaplaincy work, the geographically located parochial paradigm holds normative status for ministry. This is reflected in the fact that the chaplaincy role has no institutional traction.

In the context of the large team ministry in the Town Centre Study, complicated relational dynamics emerge between the different genres of ministry. Paul, the team rector, articulates on behalf of the team a foundational model of the relationship between chaplaincy and parish ministry and the place of chaplaincy within the mission strategy of the whole team. He sees the two ministries as having distinctive foci: 'Chaplaincy is mainly intent on making connections with folk beyond church life whereas parish life spends an awful lot of time making connections with folk through parish life' (team rector). He reflects that the primary connections in parish ministry are with people 'who actually come and worship in church', while chaplaincy primarily engages with people 'who will probably never attend your church building'. This observation points to the prosaic but fundamental point of tension noted by Brown (2011, p. 3) that 'the parish and its congregation are the basic money-raising structure on which diocesan and national activities rely for resources'. Although chaplaincy is often funded jointly or by secular organizations, this remains a significant point of tension. If the Church is to support chaplaincy in more than a notional way, it requires the Church's relationship with chaplaincy to be at least understandable on the grounds of what it contributes to its mission and ministry, if not on the more problematic grounds of what it contributes numerically or financially to the building up of the institutional Church.

Paul also described a tension between the *ad extra* missional focus of chaplaincy and the pull to focus *ad intra* experienced by many in parish ministry. In his view, the temptation for parish clergy is that they end up 'running the show' and forget that they are called to be out in the world, while for chaplains, the temptation is that they become 'almost comfortable being out in the world and so resistant to what the Church is for and about that you live your life entirely on the margins' (team rector). This fairly common view of chaplaincy as being on the margins of the Church implies a particular understanding of what the Church is for. It is grounded in an ecclesiology which understands the Church as essentially a geographically located gathered community. If this is the dominant ecclesiology, then inevitably chaplaincy will be located on the 'margins'. In contrast, a more dispersed ecclesiology which understands the primary vocation of the Church as the quest to participate in the *missio Dei* might view ministries located in society as the embodiment of the Church in the service of God's mission and therefore the engagement in social structures as being central to what the Church is for.

Given his role as team rector, it is understandable that even though Paul valued chaplaincy highly within the team, he offered a clerical-centric view of ministry and the Church which related directly to the way in which chaplaincy roles had been set up. Referring to Jesus' ministry as being spent mostly on the streets but also that he 'knew the value of a spiritual base and a spiritual home', when making chaplaincy appointments, Paul asserted the importance of appointing people who had a calling to a missional chaplaincy-type role but who also valued the life of the gathered church and wanted to have a significant role in the worshipping life of a faith community. This ecclesiology of ministry, underpinned by an implicit oppositional dualism between chaplaincy and the Church, is structurally embedded in that those appointed to the lead missional and chaplaincy roles were also made team vicars. This was seen as crucial from the Church's point of view: it was having incumbent status with a church base that validated the chaplaincy role. 'We've given the incipient authority to the role by actually making them priests of incumbent status' (team rector).

The study shows that the ecclesiology of ministry behind this approach established a particular relational dynamic between chaplaincy and church-based ministry. The fact that chaplaincy was viewed as being validated by parish ministry which was given primary status unintentionally perpetuated the tension between the ministries. One example of this is Kate's experience as town centre chaplain that it was difficult at first to convince clergy colleagues that her chaplaincy work was worthwhile. This finding confirms the contention (Boff 1977; Pickard 2009) that identifying the ecclesiologies that are at work is crucial to understanding how different ministries can work together to bear witness to the gospel. If there is to be creative dialogue between different genres of ministry, then understandings of the relationship between Church and ministry need to be made explicit, or else an often implicit dominant ecclesiology runs the risk of framing as marginal those who hold a different understanding.

A typology of the relationship between Church and ministry

A useful lens through which to analyse the data is provided by Pickard's (2009) twofold typology of the relationship between Church and ministry. The first type, often associated with the Catholic wing of the Church, emphasizes a christological approach that gives *priority to ministry over Church*. In this account, ministry precedes Church and 'the Church is constituted by a validly and divinely instituted ministerial office that has its origins in Christ's authority and institution' (p. 33). The second type gives *priority to Church and pneumatology*. Within this approach, ministry is 'an emergent *charism*-generated activity of the whole Church. The community of faith, under the guidance and inspiration of the Holy Spirit, receives and exercises the gifts of God for the common good, witness and service: the mission of the Church' (p. 36). According to Pickard, this second approach destabilizes traditional conceptions of the relationship, which have tended to prioritize the authority of ministry. He suggests that difficulties arise where the emphasis is on one or other of these approaches. Where the first is emphasized, the authority of ministerial office is accentuated and ministry can become focused on the clergy, bestowing an undue self-importance on them such that attempts to relate this ministry to other ministries inevitably diminish the latter. Where the second is emphasized, there is openness to a wide scope of lay and ordained ministries but it is difficult to achieve a proper differentiation. Pickard contends that we need to get beyond a view of ministry as separate from the collective life of the Church and to conceive the two as integrated. In this view, ministry is understood as 'action for and on behalf of the Church' and the Church is understood as 'an organic community, where ministerial differentiation contributes to and does not diminish the unity and coherence of the whole body' (p. 42).

In the Town Centre Study, the organizing approach emphasizes the priority of ministry over Church, and the implications for the relationship between the ministries is evident. In practice, because the authority of chaplaincy within the team is conceived as derivative from parish ministry, the chaplains who have a strong sense of the inherent validity of their role have to work with a structurally embodied relational dynamic that has to be constantly negotiated within the church context and the team. For example, Jenny (community missioner, police chaplain and team vicar) reflected that some colleagues referred to what she did as 'sector ministry', whereas she regarded church-based ministry as 'sector ministry', because for her the Church was the sector, rather than the rest of life. Stuart (homeless charity and team vicar) noted that team meetings tended to be about 'parish stuff' with chaplaincy seen as a 'colourful interjection', while Kate (town centre chaplain and team vicar) experienced having parish and chaplaincy roles as difficult, because church members thought they should 'have a priest to themselves'.

This tension in relation to church-based ministry only emerges where designated chaplaincy roles are differentiated. Where the work is understood as an extension of parish ministry rather than as a differentiated ministry, as in the YMCA involvement, there is no tension from the church perspective, but neither are there any parameters by virtue of which chaplaincy can be recognized as chaplaincy within the public domain. In speaking of the ecclesiology that shaped his church's vision for involvement with the YMCA, Peter talked about establishing church-related communities in specific locations outside church buildings rather than about the quest to participate in the *missio Dei*. The church's intention was to develop more of these communities, and the work in the YMCA was seen in terms of this model. The church wanted to encourage YMCA residents 'to come to a Pioneer service, a kind of Fresh Expression in the pub'. The Pioneer Minister attached to the church intended to develop his role in the YMCA by doing more visiting during the day, and this individual visiting was equated with chaplaincy work. In this instance, the parameters for chaplaincy described in Chapter 4 have not been considered. There is no differentiated chaplaincy role that is more than notionally publicly recognized and validated, and there is no appropriate accountability to the organization as well as to the faith community. Chaplaincy is described as 'an easy label' for the YMCA to understand, and Peter can see no real difference between how he might work as a chaplain and as a parish minister. In this instance, there is no conceptual clarity: none of the stakeholders are clear about what chaplaincy is.

The evidence from the case studies shows that once the theological foundations and ministerial identity of chaplaincy are described and made explicit so that it can be recognized as a distinctive genre of ministry, the issue of how it relates to the work of the whole Church in theory and in practice is brought into sharp focus. Is chaplaincy seen as a valid genre of ministry that makes a valuable contribution to the mission of the Church, or is it seen as a distraction from how the Church understands its 'core business', one which can potentially divert resources away from parish ministry?

This question resonates throughout the Market Town Study, where the church context was a much more bounded and culturally homogenous community than the plural urban context of the Town Centre Study. In this case, there is an explicit recognition of the inter-relationship between theology, ecclesiology and ministry. Beginning with the understanding that the calling of the Church is to serve the mission of God in the world, strategic thought was given to how it could engage missionally with the community in order to make a real contribution to the common good. This in turn led to the model of ministry based on functional responsibility and, within this, chaplaincy was developed as a way of engaging missionally in key areas of community life. Because chaplains had a particular focus for their ministry, they were seen as having a specialist ministry which, ideally, could not only contribute to their particular context but could also feed back into the life of the Church. In theory, this specialist role would not lead to the isolation or marginalization of the chaplain in relation to the Church but would be a conduit through which accumulated wisdom, knowledge and skills could flow between contexts. Chaplaincy roles were here seen as part of the over-all ecumenical mission strategy of the Church. Chaplaincy was recognized as a valid genre of ministry in its own right, deriving its authority within the project and the community not primarily from clerical orders or from having a particular church role but from the skill with which chaplains bore authentic witness in their role to the Christian life and tradition. This is a more integrated conception of ministry and the collective life of the Church in which, in Pickard's terms, ministerial differentiation does not diminish but contributes to the unity and coherence of the whole.

The challenges of chaplaincy

The reality, however, was that the parish was still made up of individual churches and congregations, and tensions inhabited the relationship between the chaplaincy model of ministry focused in social structures and the traditional model of ministry focused in church structures. One of the ongoing challenges in the Market Town Study was therefore to find effective ways of communicating about the chaplaincy work within the church communities. The clergy recognized the need to address church members' perceptions of chaplaincy. John (vicar) suggested that one perception might be that chaplains relieved them of any responsibility to do things, while the Methodist minister related that when a chaplain for older people was first suggested, one perception was that it was an excuse for ministers to stop visiting older people. Because the older people's chaplain worked collaboratively across the community, that anxiety was soon assuaged, but it does point to the importance of recognizing and attending to the different perceptions and anxieties there may be within church communities, however well worked out in theory a strategic vision for the relationship between the ministries may be.

Mark (team vicar and supervisor) reflected specifically on how difficult it was to integrate the chaplaincy model with day-to-day parish ministry. This was particularly the case with the further education chaplaincy, which was located within a bounded institution. He recognized that it could go on 'almost entirely divorced from the life of the parish'. His perception was that there wasn't a huge amount of interaction between the established churches based on a parochial model and the chaplaincy that they were supposed to be supporting. However, he recognized that some kind of integration was essential in order to foster a sense of the work being owned by the parish and the Methodist Church. He reflected that people in the churches may well ask, 'Why are we doing this?' and 'What do we get for our money?', so it is crucial to foster an understanding of the vision for the work. This was a big challenge given how little time ministers had to commit to an intentional process of education and integration. In Mark's view, chaplaincy also presented other challenges to the churches. Because chaplains worked in other people's structures and had to think through theologically what they were doing, he thought they had a much clearer idea about that than those working in the parish. He also thought that their understanding of a context could challenge the churches in relation to how they engage pastorally with people's lived experience. These are not comfortable challenges.

John (vicar) was well aware of the time and energy needed to implement this new way of working given the challenges that it posed and the new patterns of relating that it required. His experience was that people in the churches may not see the need for change, and even if they do, they may prefer not to embrace it given the losses that any change entails. Communication and education were recognized as key if this functional model was to work, and this was not easy. A lot of effort was put into communication through such things as articles and news sheets, but the effect depended on people being interested and reading them. In John's experience, this level of interest could not be assumed 'in a typical parish congregation where . . . a lot of people just come and worship and that's their entire commitment'. As in the Town Centre Study, chaplaincy here presented a prophetic missional challenge to congregations.

This mode of working also presents a managerial or governance challenge. Because the roles were set up outside church structures, a time-consuming proactive management approach had to be adopted in order to keep in touch and prevent them from becoming completely separate from the parish. This meant that John had less time to fulfil traditionally expected dimensions of the clergy role such as pastoral visiting. Some church members experienced this as a significant loss. The evidence from this study suggests that even within a more ecumenical ecclesiology where chaplaincy was recognized as having a valid place within the Church's ecology of mission, the relationship between the dynamics of chaplaincy and those of ministry within church structures remains challenging. John was aware that the tensions that are lived with at the parish level are mirrored, in the Anglican Church, at the national level. He reflected that if the Church is to respond effectively to cultural change by developing a mixed economy of ministry that includes chaplaincy, then the vision for ministry, its structures and priorities, will need to change. In addition, the need to provide appropriate training and support for those who initiate and drive change will have to be recognized. This represents a significant resource challenge. At the heart of this resource challenge sits the undeniable fact that parishes are the primary source of financial support for church activities. However, alongside this could be set the indicative finding from the recent Church of England chaplaincy research (Todd, Slater & Dunlop 2014, p. 17) that of the 589 full-time ordained chaplains known to the Church, 93 per cent were employed by secular organizations. John noted how the theological, cultural, financial and historical privileging of parish-based ministry in the Church of England had resulted in a history of chaplaincy posts being cut:

> Whenever there's pressure, cut the chaplaincy post, cut the stuff at the centre, and of course, all that does is leave isolated

individual ministers with no support who really do have to do everything and do things poorly because you can't do everything and be everywhere. So you do require vision at the real centre. (Vicar)

It could in fact be argued that the recent growth in chaplaincy constitutes a reclaiming by stealth of a traditional Anglican ecclesiology that understands the Church as being called to serve the whole of society. Chaplaincy evidently has a significant role to play in this respect and therefore does need to have a voice in the Church of England's current process of rethinking what its calling to serve God's mission to the whole of society in the twenty-first century implies for the structures of ministry. This is clearly a major ecclesiological challenge. The research evidence suggests the constant pull of a more or less implicit and deep-rooted dualism that locates chaplaincy as a specialist ministry in the public square that is marginal to or separate from 'the Church'. 'Chaplaincy' and 'Church' are in fact different conceptual categories that set up a false premise for dialogue. If chaplaincy and church-based ministry are rather conceptualized as distinctive but different genres of ministry within the mission and ministry of the whole Church, chaplaincy can be seen as embodying Church in the public square. This would then enable the recognition of the significant contribution it evidently makes to fulfilling the vocation of the Church to serve God's mission in the world. The narrative of chaplaincy as marginal to or on the edge of the life of the Church is, however, persistent. Chaplains are located between the gathered Church and the public arena, making connections and building bridges, and are often seen by others and self-identify as people on the boundary who occupy, according to Swift (2014), a liminal space in both the social and church structures. As I have discussed, negotiating the complexity of inhabiting this space is one of the fundamental skills of chaplaincy. Although chaplains do work across cultures and boundaries, this does not mean that the distinctive ministry that they offer is marginal to the contemporary missional concerns of the Church: this may be exactly where the Church needs to be.

If the chaplaincy narrative of marginality goes unchallenged within the churches and chaplains are perceived as marginal to their core concerns, the danger is that they become isolated and split off with an attendant lack of understanding and support from the Church. Todd (2011, p. 14) suggests that instead of this splitting, the churches could be challenged to develop an understanding of Church where chaplaincy is central to ecclesial identity rather than marginal: chaplaincy's public embodiment of Church could provide the model for the Church's wider engagement in the public square. Todd outlines the shape of this kind of ecclesiology, an outline which picks up the analysis of chaplaincy in the previous chapters. This kind of ecclesiology would:

- rely 'less on religious establishment and more on an entrepreneurial public engagement';
- work on the understanding that the Church is called to align itself with and serve the *missio Dei* and therefore 'be serious about understanding the public square in order to discover and articulate where God is at work in civil society (as well as where God's work is frustrated by human action or inaction)';
- require suspicion of some of the dualisms at work in Church and society, 'distinctions between: public and private; religious and secular; sacred and profane; spiritual and material';
- involve the Church in developing public perspectives through immersion in the public square enabling a 'critical, prophetic role';
- require being serious about dialogue and co-operation and making common cause with 'those committed to the common good including those of different faiths and beliefs'.

This kind of ecclesial perspective, modelled on chaplaincy's characteristic approach to public engagement, would, in Todd's view, help to connect the gathered Church and the public square. It would also contribute to 'an apologetic that located Christian concern for human-wellbeing as an aspect of mission, motivated by the Christian tradition'. This view therefore models Church, after chaplaincy, as a distinct, collaborative and dialogic 'way of participating in civil society'. This approach to conceptualizing ecclesial identity endorses the involvement of the whole Church in the public square just as chaplaincy supports the involvement of lay and ordained people. A shift in this direction of thinking may not be evident any time soon, but this way of thinking does at least suggest that chaplaincy has something important to say to the contemporary Church and that the development of dialogue between chaplaincy ministry and the Church could be mutually enriching and be a contribution to current thinking about mission and ministry.

A narrative of chaplaincy

The question is: what kind of narrative of chaplaincy could replace the inherited narrative of marginality and make sense to the Church? In the light of what I have said thus far, I propose that such a narrative needs to have three main strands. These three strands would represent chaplaincy as:

1 rooted in a theology of mission that locates it as central to the mission of the contemporary Church to serve God's mission in the world;
2 a distinctive ministry with its own identity and integrity that provides an important way in which the Church can live its vocation in the world;
3 rooted in an integrative ecclesiology of ministry which recognizes the interdependence of ministry and Church where ministry is understood as action for and on behalf of the Church and the Church is understood as an organic community where ministerial differentiation does not diminish but contributes to the unity and coherence of the whole.

With such an understanding, each genre of ministry can be seen as part of the 'charism-generated activity of the whole church' (Pickard 2009, p. 36). If chaplaincy is perceived in this way, it ceases to look like a valuable but ultimately dispensable genre of ministry and starts to look like one that is becoming an increasingly important part of the Church's identity and mission. It moves from being conceptualized as marginal to the Church to being conceptualized as integral and distinct.

The ecclesiology of chaplaincy discussed above seeks to understand where God is at work in the world and how to collaborate with that work. Although this understanding and the development of effective ways of working in the public square could enrich the life of the whole Church, as Mark (associate vicar) in the Market Town Study suggested, it is not clear that the Church is in a place where it can hear the challenges that chaplaincy presents. This is not new. From a historical perspective, Brown (2011, p. 6) reminds us that the contentious missiological conviction of Leslie Hunter and Ted Wickham, founders of the Industrial Mission movement in the 1940s and 1950s, was not that God was absent from working life and the Church was needed to hallow it, but that God was incarnate in human activity and that working people understood this and spoke of it in their own way. They argued that the Church was failing to connect with this 'secular theology': the mission in 'Industrial Mission' was mission to the Church. This conception of mission sought to address the theological gap between the Church and the Kingdom of God rather than the sociological gap between the Church and the world (Brown 2011). Brown suggests that in this respect, contemporary chaplaincy at its best bears a similarity to the best of Fresh Expressions which, rather than asking how to get people to come to church, asks how the Church can better reflect the nature of God to the people. The taxing question, he suggests, is whether the institutional Church really does understand its mission as this quest to participate in the *missio Dei* or whether, in its current anxiety about its survival into the future, its understanding has been captured more by secular success criteria and surrender to methods such as business models.

Conclusion

In this chapter, I have presented chaplaincy as a valuable way of being Church in the world today. As Threlfall-Holmes & Newitt

(2011b) contend, its extensive social reach offers a way of living out more comprehensively than is now possible in a purely geographically based system, the Church's vision of a universal ministry to all people. They add their voices to a call for it to be viewed as a normative and valuable part of the mission of the Church. I have argued that for this to happen, the integrity of chaplaincy as a genre of ministry needs to be described and acknowledged and the ecclesiologies and missiologies in play need to be made explicit. This groundwork has to happen for the implications for the relationships between the ministries to have a chance of being understood, so that they can be developed effectively and creatively. If the intertwining of theology, ecclesiology and ministry is not acknowledged, any tensions that there may be between the ministries have little chance of being resolved.

This kind of work and conversation is not easy. If the relationships between the ministries are to change and develop, then structures, perceptions and ways of working may have to change too. As the Market Town Study exemplifies, this can be challenging for all concerned and requires a high level of commitment and investment of energy. However, the institutional Church has recognized the need to change and diversify in order to respond faithfully to the changing culture, and it may be that it is beginning to glimpse the potential contribution of chaplaincy within its mission and ministry. One thing is clear from recent research: given the number of lay and ordained people involved in chaplaincy roles and the extensive social reach of their engagement with civil society, it is no longer tenable to portray chaplaincy as marginal to the mission and ministry of the Church.

The presentation of a narrative for chaplaincy that includes a differentiated understanding of practice not only raises the question of the relationship between different ministries, but it also raises the question of what the implications of this understanding may be for the development and support of chaplaincy practice. Chapter 6 therefore returns to a consideration of practice in the light of the understanding of chaplaincy that has been developed.

6

Doing Chaplaincy:
The Development and Support
of Chaplaincy Practice

Introduction

In April 2012, while researching chaplaincy at the Oxford Centre for Ecclesiology and Practical Theology, I organized a joint conference for practising chaplains with the British and Irish Association for Practical Theology (BIAPT). The conference was called: 'From Practice to Policy: Theological Reflection on Being a Chaplain'. There were over fifty delegates from a wide variety of contexts and a much wider expression of interest. The intention was to provide a forum in which practitioners could share experiences and have a rare opportunity to reflect theologically on practice. The opportunity to move the reflection into dialogue with the wider Church was provided by inviting Malcolm Brown, the Church of England's Director of Mission and Public Affairs, to speak.

This conference encapsulated many of the themes that have been prominent in previous chapters:

- the large number and variety of chaplaincy roles;
- the immense energy and enthusiasm of chaplains for their work;
- the lack of conceptual clarity about what 'chaplaincy' is;
- the felt lack of opportunities for theological reflection on practice;

- a sense of people often working in isolation with no awareness of the number of people doing chaplaincy and that they are part of a wide community of practice;
- the recognition of a need for training, support and development;
- a sense of chaplaincy ministry not being valued or supported in the same way as parish ministry;
- the need to engage in dialogue with the wider Church;
- the institutional Church's limited awareness of the nature and scope of contemporary chaplaincy and the contribution it makes within its ecology of mission.

This is quite a daunting list. Perhaps most importantly of all, the conference provided the opportunity for chaplains, who were sometimes working in very part-time roles, to share their experience with one another and so to find affirmation and encouragement. The basic question that was raised by the conference was: what do chaplains need in order to develop best practice?

The practice-based evidence developed from the case studies suggests that there are three main areas of need relating to practice: training; support in the development of effective and sustainable chaplaincy roles; and continuing professional development. This chapter looks briefly at each of these areas and offers suggestions that are intended to encourage dialogue and to spark further ideas for the development and support of best and faithful practice.

Chaplaincy training

The picture of training provision for chaplaincy in community contexts is complex and varied to the extent that it is impossible to gain an accurate picture of what is available. At one level, there is a significant amount of academic interest in this public ministry ranging from university research to people undertaking doctorates and Master's degrees in chaplaincy. There are also modules on chaplaincy nestling within various MA and DMin degrees. Any search for training courses on the internet will locate a diverse selection of postgraduate courses relating to chaplaincy, although they are mainly for people working in institutional contexts such as schools, prisons, healthcare and the armed forces. At a less academic level, several of the different chaplaincy contexts organize their own network support and training. Some of this is voluntary and informal, some mandatory and 'professional' as with the police. However, there is no specific accredited training available to lay and ordained people in authorized ministry who develop chaplaincy roles or who find that chaplaincy is a required component of their church-based role. In the Church of England, a significant percentage of parish clergy will at some point in their ministry find themselves occupying chaplaincy-type roles by choice or otherwise. As discussed previously, there are no accurate statistics for this, but an estimate would be between 10 and 15 per cent of Anglican clergy, although it may be higher than this. There is a need for accessible basic training for such roles, given that many of them will be undertaken in controlled environments such as schools, colleges or care homes where, apart from any other considerations, safe and ethical working practices need to be assured.

First of all, I therefore suggest that chaplaincy ministry needs to be thought about in relation to the selection of people for ministerial training. If chaplaincy is to find its identity and integrity within the mission and ministry of the Church, the training needs of different categories of people need to be thought about. Some people do have a calling to chaplaincy rather than parish ministry, as evidenced by Kate, the town centre chaplain. At present, there is no recognized training pathway designed to support chaplaincy ministry. Even though some people are accepted for training as Pioneer Ministers, the normative assumption, at least in the Church of England, is that all ministerial training is for parish ministry. Once people begin training, the norm is that they are trained for parish ministry even though, as already discussed, this paradigm is shifting and may be becoming unsustainable in its current form. Ordinands may be able to do a placement in a chaplaincy context, but there are no specific courses to equip people for chaplaincy ministry.

One positive sign that this situation could change is that the Church of England has recently developed a new ministerial training curriculum accredited by Durham University called the Common Awards.[1] This does provide a module on chaplaincy that training institutions can choose to offer as a one-week special interest course. This is a small step forward. At least chaplaincy is recognized as a genre of ministry within the curriculum, but it still leaves it as a semi-detached option. When I and a colleague, John Caperon, wrote the outline for this module, the hope was that it might be a useful introduction for people in ministerial training who wish to explore chaplaincy as a future option or to confirm their commitment to it as a genre of ministry. However, a week's course which provides space to experience and reflect on chaplaincy can only be an introduction; it is not a training course for chaplaincy ministry. Assuming that some training institutions opt to offer the module, the students who opt to take it and then go on to develop chaplaincy work will currently find that there are no obvious resources provided by the Church for training and professional development in chaplaincy ministry.

It is important to say at this point that the 2014 report on Church of England involvement in chaplaincy (Todd, Slater & Dunlop) recognized the strategic importance of whole or part-time employed co-ordinating chaplains who are usually ordained, such as in police or commercial sector chaplaincy. It is these people who can be the catalyst for developing and sustaining chaplaincy teams comprising lay and volunteer (lay and ordained) chaplains as reflected in the figures for the potential number of chaplains referred to in Chapter 1. These lay and volunteer chaplains constitute a major resource in chaplaincy and need to be provided with relevant training and support. For those who work in a team, training relevant to the context will usually be provided by the co-ordinating chaplain, but not everyone works in a team which enables them to access relevant training. As mentioned in the Introduction, the need to provide accessible training resources

---

1 The website for this can be accessed at: www.dur.ac.uk/common. awards/.

for a wide cross-section of people who may become involved in chaplaincy has been recognized by the Methodist Church of Great Britain and is reflected in its development of the Chaplaincy Everywhere Course as a resource for congregations that want to think about this ministry.

It is clearly the case that people working in established chaplaincy contexts such as the prison service and NHS Trusts and for institutions such as the police do have opportunities for training and development. However, my involvement in chaplaincy research over the past five years has led me to believe that at the moment, practitioners already working as chaplains in the community, for example in care and nursing homes, constitute a second group of people who could benefit from opportunities for training and development so that they can develop best practice and feel affirmed and supported in what they are doing. Many chaplains in community roles work part-time, some for just a few hours a week, and it can be easy to feel isolated in such roles. There is a need for people to be able to come together, to exchange experiences and reflections so that they can recognize themselves as part of an extensive community of practice that makes an important contribution to the Church's mission.

For the Church of England, the relationship with chaplains is markedly different in each diocese. However, the growing recognition of the potential value of chaplaincy as a way for faith and belief groups to engage in the public square poses the question of how the churches might appropriately support those who minister in their name. One approach might be the development of an accredited Certificate in Chaplaincy, which could provide an accessible basic qualification in chaplaincy that would ensure, recognize and affirm people's skills and competence to practise.

A third group of people who might welcome training and support are those in ministry teams who want to develop chaplaincy ministry as part of missional engagement with the community. The case studies presented here have shown that this can be a complicated and time-consuming process, and my experience of supporting people in the development of such roles bears this out. In order to enable people to benefit from the experience of others,

I therefore outline a developmental consultancy model for chaplaincy which may be used by individuals who have already initiated a role or with teams or groups to provide support in moving through the process of chaplaincy development. This model was originally developed for use by people based in the community, but those in established chaplaincy roles could also find the process helpful in developing their work. The approach is likely to be relevant given that chaplains increasingly need to work across the boundaries between institutions and the community as in mental health chaplaincy and end of life care.

The development of effective and sustainable chaplaincy roles: a practical developmental consultancy model for chaplaincy

Many chaplaincy roles in community contexts begin as an entrepreneurial or pastoral response to a perceived need in a particular context, as exemplified in the Rural Benefice Study. However, as involvement grows, people can begin to feel isolated in the work. They often have no opportunities to reflect with others on the work, have no access to models of best practice, and find that their ministry in social structures may not be well supported or understood in the church context with which they are involved. For some people, it is also the case that their role may not be fully understood in the social context of their work, and, as we have seen, some people in designated chaplaincy roles do not have a clear idea of what chaplaincy is themselves. The evidence has shown that in order for chaplaincy to be sustainable and effective, people need to be able to give an account of what, how and why they are doing what they are doing. In order to be able to do that, thought needs to be given to what the role entails, the theological rationale for it, the need for training, support and supervision, and the establishment of clear lines of accountability.

Chapter 4 set out some parameters developed from the research within which chaplaincy praxis can be described and recognized as such. These are summarized in Table 1 below and constitute a conceptual basis for dialogue and thinking about chaplaincy.

The consultancy model, developed in 2011, proposes the use of these basic dimensions to provide a structure to support people who wish to develop chaplaincy through a process of reflection. The purpose is to enable people to think through the practical, professional and theological issues involved in developing chaplaincy practice, recognizing the integrity of chaplaincy as a genre of ministry and its significance within the mission of the wider Church. This in turn will give the best chance for effective and sustainable chaplaincy roles to be established and so for the Church to collaborate with God's ongoing creative work in the world. One of the inspiring things about chaplaincy is that it is for the whole Church, lay and ordained, paid and voluntary. This means that there is a wide spectrum of people with different gifts and resources who may feel called to explore this ministry. It also lends itself to ecumenical working, as in the Market Town Study. It is a

Dimension	Main Characteristics
Theological Integrity	Focus on: • serving the *missio Dei*; • building up the Kingdom of God; • contributing to human and social flourishing and the common good.
Ministerial Identity	• Representative role focusing the vocation of the Church to serve God's mission in the world; • embedded in social structures; • publicly recognized and validated; • appropriately accountable to host context and faith community.
Professional Integrity	• works in a professional way in order to offer a knowledgeable, skilled and contextually responsive ministry.

Table 1: Dimensions of chaplaincy praxis.

way in which the different churches in an area can come together to consider how best to serve God's mission in the community. By the end of the process, the basic dimensions of chaplaincy will have been addressed. The process set out below therefore offers a series of ten steps with basic questions that can be adapted and/or augmented for use in local circumstances. The assumption is that this process will be undertaken in a context of ongoing prayerful discernment, and ideally with a consultant who understands chaplaincy and can guide and support people through the process.

Step 1: Preliminary considerations

What is the motivation for considering the development of chaplaincy?

Is the motivation theological, pastoral, missional, pragmatic, financial, or a mixture of these? Is it a response to a specific need or request? How are you going to articulate the motivation as you understand it at the moment? Do you need a process for discussing/discerning this? Do you need a process for communicating it with others and gaining feedback?

What do you want to achieve?

You may have very clear ideas about what you want to achieve at the beginning, or you may have just a general idea that you want to develop the Church's presence and engagement in the local community. Even if you are not clear, it is a good idea at this stage to think about what you want to achieve and to try to be as clear as possible, as this will provide focus and impetus for the process. When you have done this, try to identify some specific goals. You may find it helpful to have someone to work alongside you to help you to do this. You are more likely to achieve your goals, however modest they are, if they are clear, so it is well worth taking some time to do this. You may be aware of the SMART acronym that is often used to guide people through this process. Goals need to be:

- Specific.
- Measurable (how will I know that I have achieved the goal?).
- Achievable.
- Realistic.
- Timed (what is the timescale?).

Remember, nothing is set in stone, and your ideas and goals may well change as the process progresses, and you gain more information and insight. The resources that you can access may also change and affect the process.

What kind of theological understanding of the work do you have?

How does your understanding of chaplaincy relate to the discernment of God's mission in the world? How can this understanding be communicated with those who need to understand why it is important to develop this work? Take time to articulate the theological rationale for the work, as this underpins the whole initiative.

Who is going to provide leadership in developing a chaplaincy initiative?

If the process is to be effective, it is important to identify who is going to provide leadership and take responsibility for enabling people to move through the process. Think about how this process needs to be undertaken in your context.

Who are the potential stakeholders in the proposed or existing initiative?

People need to think about all those who may have an actual or potential stake in developing this ministry. As we have seen, this may include not only those directly involved in any initiative but also, for example, members of the church and the local community.

Although understandings and motivations may change and develop through the process, it is important to begin by considering these questions so that the foundations for the work are made explicit at the beginning. It is important to be as clear as you can be about *why* you are entering into this process and that people have the chance to reflect and comment on this. This will help to develop commitment to the process and to the implementation of its outcomes.

Step 2: Listen to and understand the context

What is going on in this context?

What is happening in the social, cultural and ecclesial context both locally and more widely? In the local context, what, when and where do things happen? Who is involved? What is positive and what might need to change or be developed? Although listening is the essential mode of engagement throughout the process, it is particularly important at Step 2 in order to gain as full and deep an understanding of the context as possible. This is the foundation for any development. Take time to try and understand and describe every aspect of your context as fully as possible. Talk to people, listen to people.

How are you listening?

- To what the situation is saying?
- To what the people that you meet are saying?
- To what God might be saying and doing?
- To yourselves as individuals and as a community?
- To one another as you go through this process?

Step 3: Take stock of the current situation

What existing connections and relationships do people have?

It is always a good idea to start from wherever you are! However, sometimes the obvious can be overlooked due to familiarity. It is worth asking who already has a relationship or connections in the community. For example, someone may have a relative in a care home whom they visit regularly and in so doing has built up good relationships with other residents and staff.

What opportunities exist for involvement in community contexts?

The case studies provide several examples of chaplaincy development in response to the discernment of opportunities for involvement. Good examples of this would be the work with older people or with the further education college in the Market Town Study.

What is already happening in this context?

It is important to know what is happening already so that existing work is not duplicated or even jeopardized and an appropriate response is made. Are there existing chaplaincies around, for example, healthcare, prisons, town centre, care homes, the police? Listen to and talk with people involved in such chaplaincies. Would it be appropriate to offer to support them with personnel, prayer or financial resources? Think carefully about how and where God might be calling you to get involved.

The process in Step 3 can help you decide what response you want to make in your situation and the kind of chaplaincy involvement that it might be appropriate to develop. Once you have found a focus, Step 4 can help you to think more specifically about chaplaincy ministry.

Step 4: Describe the model of chaplaincy being or to be used

What is 'chaplaincy'?

It is important to describe for everyone involved what you mean by chaplaincy. Do not take it for granted that people have a common understanding of the term. The dimensions of chaplaincy summarized above in Table 1 can help you to do this.

What does/will chaplaincy look like in your context?

Think back to what was said about the dialogic nature of chaplaincy in Chapter 1. What are the different contexts and cultures with which the chaplaincy you are thinking about will need to be in dialogue? What kind of chaplaincy response is needed? Will it require, for example, a single person, a team, lay or ordained people, or a mixture of both? Paid or voluntary; if paid, then by whom? Build up as full a description as you can of what you think the chaplaincy needs to look like. This will include the kind of approach needed in a particular context. Think about the different gifts and qualities that may be required. For example, the gifts, skills and approach needed in a further education college will be different from those needed in a nursing home or working with homeless people.

Step 5: Articulate a vision for the work

What is your vision for the work?

By this stage you will have thought about what you feel called to engage with and the kind of chaplaincy that could enable you to do that effectively. Now, spend some time setting out your vision for the work: why you want to do it, how you might go about doing it, and what you hope to achieve either in the short, medium or longer term. How can you make that vision explicit and communicate it effectively? Who needs to know about this vision?

Also, think about how you hold the vision that is being born. Are you holding it lightly and provisionally or rigidly and possessively? Are you open to it being changed and developed as you engage in dialogue with others, especially those whom you seek to serve?

Step 6: Negotiating a chaplaincy role

What have you decided to do?

By Step 6 you should have a good idea of what the needs and opportunities are in your context and so be equipped to decide on the kind of chaplaincy involvement to explore. Remember that chaplains are invited guests who work within other people's structures. They need to negotiate their presence in a context, as in the example of the development of the further education chaplaincy post in the Market Town Study. The process will have helped you to clarify why you want to develop this work, what you have to offer and your understanding of the chaplaincy role.

What conversations do you need to have?

You will need to identify the main stakeholders in the particular context and decide what conversations you need to open in order to begin to negotiate. It may be that you have already identified existing connections and relationships that provide a natural opening to a context or organization. It is important to pay attention to the kind of language and approach that you use. Although many organizations and contexts may be open to an approach about chaplaincy, they will want to know how it will benefit the organization and its 'clients'. Why would they want to have a chaplain? What value would chaplaincy bring? Think carefully about how chaplaincy would contribute to the mission of the host organization as well as to the mission of the Church.

Step 7: Establish an effective and sustainable chaplaincy practice

What resources do you need to establish the role?

Chapter 4 argued that if a chaplaincy is to be effective and sustainable, then chaplains need to work in a professional way. It sets out the elements of professional chaplaincy practice. The resources required to do this need to be identified. What personnel are required? You will need to think about the recruitment process. This will include having a job description, a person specification and an application form which provides information about the applicants' gifts and skills and why they want to apply. The job description needs to be clear about how the appointee will be accountable in both the host organization and the church context. Applicants then need to be interviewed. You will also need to collect references and pay appropriate attention to Safeguarding issues. The human resource processes that you put in place should apply to both voluntary and paid roles. Chaplains minister in the public square and need to go through an appropriate selection process so that everyone involved can have confidence that the ministry will be undertaken in a professional way. This process may need to be ongoing, especially if you need to maintain a certain number of volunteers.

What resources do you need to sustain the role?

How are ongoing supervision, support, training and development going to be provided? Will there be opportunities for chaplains to reflect on their practice? What physical, spiritual and emotional resources are required? How will the role be evaluated?

What structures need to be put in place for selection, co-ordination, support and training? What resources are available?

Are there appropriate structures, procedures, training and resources to sustain the work? If not, what steps can you take to improve this situation?

Step 8: Describe and evaluate current practice (for practising chaplains)

What is your current practice?

If you are already involved in providing chaplaincy, describe your current practice. How does what you describe relate to your understanding of chaplaincy? How does it relate to what you learn in dialogue with others? What would best practice look like in your context? What do you need in order to offer and sustain best practice? How can you find what you need? Who could help you?

Step 9: Listen to those you seek to serve

Are the voices of those you seek to serve being heard?

Are you able and willing to listen to those voices so that you can understand what kind of a response is needed? What structures and processes do you need to put in place so that they can be heard? Are you willing to enter into genuine dialogue with others, recognizing that you have things to learn from each other and that you need to be prepared to be changed by the encounters?

Step 10: Attend to the relationship of chaplaincy with the wider ministerial context

What kind of governance is appropriate?

Are mediating structures required such as a chaplaincy steering, development or support group? How is chaplaincy reviewed? Is there an appraisal system in place?

What does chaplaincy bring to the church context and vice versa?

If people in the church context are to understand and support chaplaincy ministry, there needs to be effective communication about the work. Can those involved be encouraged or trained to reflect theologically on practice in order to develop an understanding of chaplaincy as a distinctive genre of ministry that is integral to the Church's ecology of mission? How can pathways of mutual enrichment, insight and growth be developed? What opportunities are there for chaplains and those in parish-based ministry to engage in dialogue or conversation?

In summary, these are the ten key questions to keep in mind:

Step 1: What do I/we want to achieve and why?

Step 2: What is my/our understanding of the context?

Step 3: How can we engage with this context?

Step 4: What is chaplaincy and what will it look like in this context?

Step 5: What is my/our vision for the work?

Step 6: What will I/we do?

Step 7: What resources are needed?

Step 8: What is my/our current practice and what do I/we need to develop it? (For practising chaplains.)

Step 9: How do I/we listen to those I/we seek to serve?

Step 10: How does chaplaincy ministry relate to the wider ministerial context?

Using the Ten-step Consultancy Model

This ten-step model is a suggested process that can be adapted and used to suit local circumstances. If there is already chaplaincy involvement in the community, it can be used as a reflective tool to develop practice, or it may be used by an individual chaplain as a way of reviewing his or her work with a supervisor. Not all of it will be appropriate to every situation, and for some people it may represent a model for good practice that can be worked towards. People need to use it in their situation in a way that works for them. The questions will not necessarily be addressed consecutively or in the exact order that they are set out above, and you may find yourself going backwards and forwards between questions and revisiting certain questions at different points during the process. It is a *developmental* model that begins and ends with practice, and an iterative process which invites people to stay open to listening and learning throughout. Ideas, understandings and goals may well change until you decide what you are going to do. As with all best practice, whatever is set up will then need to be reviewed and changed in response to further reflection on practice. However, although this is an open spiral process, if followed, the steps can enable you to develop understanding of why you want to develop chaplaincy and what you want to achieve, conceptual clarity about chaplaincy, understanding of the theological rationale for chaplaincy ministry, and a framework for establishing effective and sustainable chaplaincy practice.

Continuing Professional Development (CPD)

The introduction to this chapter identified the third area of need relating to chaplaincy practice as continuing professional development. Although chaplains in established roles may have opportunities for CPD, there is scant literature or research relating to the development and support of chaplaincy practice more widely. Over the past five years I have listened to chaplains working across a wide variety of contexts both individually and at conferences such as the one described at the beginning of this chapter and at several BIAPT conferences. The feedback that I have received from them leads me to conclude that there are limited opportunities for people to reflect theologically on practice with other chaplains. When this kind of reflection has been facilitated, chaplains have fed back that it has helped them to think about the development of their practice. Through my research and work with chaplains, I have identified five areas of work that could be developed to provide a framework for CPD for authorized ministers working as chaplains.

Theological reflection on practice and pastoral supervision

Although discussions about theological reflection and pastoral supervision may be well-trodden ground (Thompson, Pattison & Thompson 2008; Leach & Paterson 2010), it is well worth highlighting the value of these practices in relation to the development of chaplaincy. Across the country, there are established chaplaincy teams where chaplains do have regular supervision and the opportunity to reflect together on practice, but I am also aware of a number of teams who do not engage in any kind of formal reflective practice. I am also aware that there are many chaplains working on their own or in community contexts who have no access to this kind of developmental practice. I have argued that one of the reasons why chaplaincy in the community has hitherto lacked a voice or recognition within the central ministerial and missiological discourses of the Church is that there has been limited reflection on practice with the opportunity that this brings to develop thinking, practice and ministerial identity.

Theological reflection

In Chapter 4 I argued that if the identity and integrity of chaplaincy ministry is to be established, chaplains need to work in a professional and ethical way. This means that there needs to be appropriate accountability in both the host context and the church context and there needs to be ongoing support. As for anyone who works in a professional way, time needs to be factored into working hours for reflection on practice as a way of learning from experience. This has become a fundamental component of professional training and development, particularly in education and nursing through the use of Kolb's experiential learning cycle (1983). This model of learning provides the space for practitioners to consciously stand back from their engagement in practice in order to be able to reflect on it in a structured way. This in turn enables the practitioner to deepen insight or develop new insight that can in turn feed into the development or even the transformation of practice. The experiential learning cycle has four basic stages which, ideally, flow into one another in a perpetual spiral of learning:

1 Identification of a specific experience.
2 Reflecting on the experience at one remove as an observer rather than an actor.
3 Deriving and applying general rules, principles or concepts from the experience.
4 Trying out new ways of acting in the light of new insights and choices that emerge.

The pastoral cycle of reflection has been developed from Kolb's experiential cycle of learning, the key difference being that it makes space for the incorporation of theological insight from the faith tradition of the practitioner. A useful summary of different models of theological reflection can be found in the *SCM Study Guide to Theological Reflection* (Thompson, Pattison & Thompson 2008), and an example of its use in practice is described in *Theological Reflection for Human Flourishing* (Cameron et al. 2012). The basic hermeneutic process of this theological reflection cycle involves:

1 Identification of a specific experience/issue.
2 Building a multi-layered or 'thick' description from a variety of perspectives.

3 Critical reflection drawing on different perspectives, for example sociological, theological, economic, psychological.
4 Engaging in dialogue with the relevant faith tradition.
5 Allowing time and space for new insight and understanding to emerge.
6 Deciding on and planning action in the light of what has emerged.
7 Implementing the course of action.
8 Beginning another cycle of reflection.

As faithful practitioners in the world, we need continually to review what we are doing, why we are doing it and whether we are doing it in the most effective and creative way. It is part of being faithful stewards of the available resources. Theological reflection on practice also provides the space in which we can attend and listen to ourselves, our context, the faith tradition and God, 'in the hope and expectation that the Holy Spirit will continually reveal new things if we dare to look and have eyes to see and hearts to respond . . . it is a graced process that can help us to see more clearly how we might participate in God's unfolding purpose for the world' (Cameron et al. 2012, p. 9). This process is a valuable learning and practice development tool that is best undertaken in a group or at least with one other person. However, it is not just about what we do in our work but also about nurturing our identity and understanding of who we are as people of faith, and how that understanding is expressed as transformative action and presence in the world.

Supervision

Supervision is a well-established component of working in a professional and ethical way. It provides the opportunity for both support and accountability and, if used well, can enable the development of competence, confidence and creativity. There are many different and helpful models of supervision in secular practice (Carroll & Tholstrup 2001; Hawkins & Shohet 2000) which can benefit people in ministry. In *Pastoral Supervision: A Handbook* (2010), Leach and Paterson describe an approach to supervision which begins in prayer and Scripture but is open to insights from other approaches. Theological reflection on practice is integral to this approach which is described by Leach & Paterson as

> a relationship between two or more disciples who meet to consider the ministry of one or more of them in an intentional and disciplined way. This provides the space for each supervisee to give an account of their work, to explore their responses, review their aims, and develop their strategies and skills.

Pastoral supervision is undertaken in order to support the well being, growth and development of the supervisee and for the sake of those among whom they work as it provides 'a realistic point of accountability within the body of Christ for their work' (Leach & Paterson 2010, p. 1). The more recent *Enriching Ministry: Pastoral Supervision in Practice* (Rose & Paterson 2014) offers a wider ranging overview of pastoral supervision, its relationship with other disciplines and fields of study and its potential as a practice for supporting, enriching and energizing ministry.

This may be a creative approach for people in ministry, but as with most things in chaplaincy, appropriate supervisory arrangements will need to be worked out according to the local context and resources. An example from the research is Clare, the older person's chaplain, who had regular supervision with the Methodist minister. If chaplains are employed by a secular organization, it may be that the organization provides some kind of required supervision. For example, in my own current practice in the NHS, I have on alternate months individual clinical supervision and group supervision with my immediate team, both with an external supervisor. However it is provided, in order to work in a professional way, supervision for chaplains needs to be thought about and developed as part of the necessary structures of support and accountability. This may not be easy. Although organizations like the Association for Pastoral Supervisors and Educators

(APSE)[2] do provide a network of supervisors, these are few and far between and busy part-time chaplains may not be able to access such resources. This raises the difficult questions of how opportunities for theological reflection on practice and/or pastoral supervision can be made available in an accessible way to lay and ordained chaplains working in community contexts, and of what part the churches might have to play in such provision.

The development of a community of practice

The significance and potential of the diversity of chaplaincy ministry within the mission of the Church hitherto has not been fully acknowledged by the institution, and the identity and integrity of modern community-based chaplaincy has not been adequately described. This has led to a situation in which, particularly though not exclusively, for many emerging roles, structures of support, supervision and accountability may not have been thought about explicitly. Until the significance, identity and integrity of chaplaincy are discussed and reflected upon, issues of training, support and accountability can often remain optional items on the agenda for developing roles. One way of addressing this might be to develop a community or network of chaplaincy practice within which chaplains from diverse contexts could meet together. The Methodist Church has already established a virtual forum[3] to address something of this need, but the need to make connections that has been a theme throughout this book suggests that actual meetings could be both supportive and productive. These could take place at particular centres with an interest in the support and development of chaplaincy ministry. Such meetings would enable people to reflect together theologically on practice, give and receive support and affirmation, and share experience, information, research, resources and best practice.

---

2 The APSE website can be accessed at www.pastoralsupervision.org.uk.
3 www.opensourcechaplaincy.org.uk.

Part of the development of a community of learning and support would include the creation of accessible learning resources and an accredited course based on practice that would assure, affirm and develop competence in chaplaincy ministry. It may also be possible to identify experienced chaplains who could provide consultancy, coaching and mentoring for people developing chaplaincy roles. This may sound unrealistic given the current financial constraints under which we all work. However, not only do different faiths now recognize the significance of and need for chaplaincy, but secular organizations do too. I currently work within the Department of Chaplaincy and Pastoral Care in an NHS Trust where Macmillan Cancer Support has financed a new pilot project. Three half-time posts have been funded for 18 months to provide specialist spiritual and pastoral care for adult cancer patients and those who care for them. This initiative recognizes the importance of spiritual and pastoral care to the large and increasing number of people living with cancer. The fact that a major national charity recognizes the importance of this ministry as a way of meeting and supporting people where they are in their lives must have something to say to the churches. What is the Church's vision for this kind of work in the community? How can it work in partnership with secular organizations and networks in order to serve the local community through chaplaincy ministry? People wrestling with such questions might well benefit from being able to share the experience and expertise to be found within a community of practice.

Research

The current interest in chaplaincy as public ministry is reflected in the development of chaplaincy studies as a field of research. Chaplaincy research is being undertaken in academic institutions such as the Cardiff Centre for Chaplaincy Studies, within public sector chaplaincy such as Healthcare and by other institutions such as the think-tank Theos. This is motivated by the common perception, discussed in previous chapters, that this is a growing area of public engagement for faith and belief groups with the potential to promote the common good but which hitherto has been given minimal attention. The increasing awareness of the potential of chaplaincy in the service of civil society is signalled by the publication of *A Handbook of Chaplaincy Studies: Understanding Spiritual Care in Public Places* (Swift, Cobb & Todd 2015). However, at this time of economic constraint, those who pay for chaplaincy services want to know what value chaplaincy adds and what it contributes to desired outcomes (Handzo, Cobb et al. 2014). Chaplains who work in the public sector are well aware of the need to provide evidence of the impact and value of what they do and therefore that research awareness is essential to the development both of services and of best practice (Slater 2015). For example, my current role is part of a new pilot project. The team is therefore required to gather both quantitative data about activity such as the number of patients visited, the level of interaction and the demand, and qualitative data through feedback on the service from patients, carers and staff. This feedback enables the team to gain an overview of the impact of the practice and to understand what might need to be changed or developed so that the service can best fulfil its original aim and purpose. The information will also provide the evidence upon which an evaluation of the impact of the service can be undertaken. The generation of this kind of evidence is crucial when questions about the support and resourcing of a service are in question – which they nearly always are.

Chaplains working in different contexts obviously need to find ways of establishing practice-based evidence that works in their particular setting. Whatever the context, once a service is being provided, it is necessary to keep in review the aim and purpose of the work. This will determine the kind of quantitative and qualitative evidence that needs to be generated in order to assess the impact of the work and support the development of the service.

This is important work and it is important that this research base continues to grow and to be strengthened. However, most of the research attends to public sector chaplaincy where, although resources may be tight, there is a professional ethos of research awareness and a developing recognition of the need to develop practice-based evidence. Less attention has been given to the kinds of chaplaincy roles undertaken by ministers in the community as represented in the research in this book. Research in this area of practice is equally necessary. If chaplaincy is to flourish and establish its identity and integrity as a genre of ministry, there is an urgent need to build up a body of research which can provide an evidence base for its impact and effectiveness. Apart from anything else, such work is needed to provide the basis for securing resources for chaplaincy either from the churches or from partnership organizations.

Case study research can be one powerful way in which to focus on a particular area of practice in order to generate practical knowledge that can inform both practice and policy development (Slater 2015). This approach is described at the beginning of Chapter 2. The Methodist Church has developed a different model for collecting qualitative data in conjunction with the University of Bristol as part of the Chaplaincy Everywhere project. Called the Mug of Tea (MoT) approach,[4] it is based on the gathering of short stories (in the time it takes to share a mug of tea) about an area of chaplaincy involvement from different people within an organization. The stories are recorded, transcribed and reflected upon by a neutral person who seeks to detect the Most Significant Change (MSC) that emerges from each story. The findings can then be discussed between chaplains and stakeholders. If done well, this process can enhance transparency and accountability and promote collaboration between chaplains and the structures within which they work. In the 2015 Theos report on chaplaincy, Ryan (2015) notes this model and suggests that it may be appropriate to include faith and belief group stakeholders in the same or a parallel process so that they too can assess the impact of their chaplains against their mission and purpose. He suggests that at least they ought to adapt a similar process as a

---

4 A description of this model can be found at www.opensourcechaplaincy.org.uk/chaplaincy-everywhere/.

way of engaging with, supporting and resourcing the asset that is chaplaincy. If a community of practice were to be established, this could provide a context within which research awareness could be developed, and the use and effectiveness of different models and approaches could be explored. This might encourage and support practitioners in finding appropriate ways to evaluate their practice and to participate in the development of practice-based evidence.

Conclusion

This chapter has tried to make clear some of the practical implications involved in developing chaplaincy ministry in community contexts. The care with which this needs to be done reflects an *a priori* understanding of the theological and practical significance of this contemporary practice. What will have become clear is the fact that the setting up of such roles takes time, energy, resources and commitment. It requires theological reflection, discernment, research, clear practical thinking and good communication. There are many challenges involved in setting up and undertaking this work but these challenges, if approached with care and support, can be exciting and energizing.

My experience of talking with chaplains is that they are, almost without exception, full of enthusiasm for their work and eager to share ideas for its development. There is a lot of energy in chaplaincy, energy that needs to be valued and nurtured both by the institutional Church and by the community of chaplaincy practitioners. There is currently a lot of concern about church growth within the Church of England, and no doubt within other denominations. It may be that chaplaincy as a Spirit-led ecclesial response to a changing world is a creative, growing dimension of the Church that has not been recognized as such because it eludes the current dominant preoccupations of the institution. This is its strength and its challenge. In order to be seen in this light, understandings of Church, of mission and of ministry need to be rethought and enlarged. This constitutes a considerable challenge to the churches. It is also a challenge to everyone involved with chaplaincy and everyone who recognizes the significance of this ministry in the twenty-first century. There is a great deal of work to be done.

Conclusion:
Questions and Challenges
for the Future

As practical theology this book has tried to root what it has to say in the lived experience of those engaged in chaplaincy ministry. The case studies have provided a conduit for the voices of some of those chaplains to be heard. This is important for several reasons. First of all, it guarantees that what has been said is anchored in ministerial experience and is based on a commitment to a careful listening to chaplains over several years. Second, it has enabled the legitimate prioritization of the voices of chaplains in an ecclesial context where it is difficult for those voices to be heard. This does not mean that any other form of ministry is devalued in any way. It simply means that, given the understandable historical and institutional dominance of parish ministry, in order to be heard within the institution, the voice of chaplaincy needs to find places where it can be affirmed and privileged so that those who are called to exercise this ministry have opportunity to fulfil their vocation confidently with acknowledgement of the support and resources that they need.

The Westminster Debate[1] on the future of the parochial system held in Oxford in October 2014 is just one indication that the Church of England has recognized that the system is not sustainable in its current form and that something will have to change. Hitherto, chaplaincy has not been on the radar as a potential part of that change. This book has explored why that might be the case. The case studies are by their very nature a snapshot in time; nearly all the participants have now either moved on or retired from their posts. However, what they have helped to reveal is that the contextually responsive ministry that is chaplaincy is alive and flourishing and that it may offer a hopeful way for the churches to fulfil their vocation to serve God's mission in the world in the twenty-first century. The entrepreneurial theology and social engagement characteristic of chaplaincy ministry seems to be particularly suited to the contemporary fluid and plural cultural context. This approach was affirmed in the Westminster Debate by Lord Andrew Mawson OBE, a URC minister and one of the UK's leading social entrepreneurs. He stressed that what is needed in the churches is entrepreneurial leadership, people who can recognize and seize opportunities to work in partnership with others in the community to create something of lasting value that contributes to human flourishing and the common good.

This approach resonates with Spencer's missional paradigm of 'finding hope in local communities' and with chaplaincy ministry. This is not to say that people in different forms of ministry do not work in partnership with the local community, but it is to say that this kind of approach is particularly characteristic of chaplaincy. As I have discussed, chaplaincy begins where people are, it listens and builds relationships of trust as the basis for pastoral care and prophetic witness. It draws on the resources and values of the faith tradition in order to support human and social flourishing and the common good in particular contexts in alignment with

---

1 The debate was organized by Linda Woodhead (Professor of Sociology of Religion at Lancaster University) and Martyn Percy (former Principal of Ripon College Cuddesdon, currently Dean of Christ Church Cathedral, Oxford). For further information see www.faithdebates.org.uk/oxford.

God's ongoing mission for the healing of the whole Creation. The experience of chaplains who work in this way has the potential to enrich the life and witness of the gathered Church if ways can be found for genuine dialogue to take place.

One particular contribution that chaplaincy could make within the mission of the Church is the sharing of the experience of chaplains in their engagement with and understanding of contemporary spirituality as described in Chapter 1. Tacey's analysis that the historic emphasis on institutions and beliefs is being replaced by a focus on the pragmatic and experiential elements of faith certainly resonates with my own experience of listening to people as a healthcare chaplain over the past two decades and with that of the chaplains in the case studies. He goes on to suggest that what we are seeing in the growth in interest in spirituality is the stirrings of spirit 'without the social institutions of forms in which spirit can be clearly recognized' (2012, p. 477). In an article for the World Community for Christian Meditation newsletter, referring to the institutional Church, he reflects that it may be the case that 'the world has replaced church as the consecrated vessel of the divine' and that 'Religiousness is no longer synonymous with attending holy places on holy days, but cultivating an awareness of the presence of the holy in creation, and becoming attuned to it as a discipline of mind and behaviour' (Tacey 2014, pp. 7–8). If it is true, as Tacey contends, that spirit is resurgent in the community, outside traditional structures, then chaplaincy is ideally placed to discern the movements of the spirit, located as it is in social structures. In this view, 'everything is potentially filled with the sacred, whereas once it was safely contained and kept in order' (Tacey 2012, p. 477). This, of course, may fill traditional institutions with anxiety, but if attended to fully, it may turn out to be the source of the hope that chaplaincy seeks to find and to nurture in local communities, an understanding of which could enrich the life of the whole Church.

There is a wide consensus that the mainstream denominations in England are facing particular challenges at this time in response to a changing culture of which the rise of spirituality is a constituent part. Although pockets of vibrancy undoubtedly exist, such as the growth in cathedral congregations that is regularly cited, over-all, membership is declining. Even the evidence for growth in atten-dance at cathedrals is contentious. Recent research into church growth by the Church of England (Archbishops' Council 2014) found that 74 per cent of participants who had started to attend a cathedral over the past five years were already 'churched' when they began to do so; that is, they were transferring from another church or joining the cathedral while continuing to worship at another church. At the same time as this decline in membership, the social demographic is changing with an increase of elderly people in the population, a large cohort of clergy approaching retirement, pressure on resources and the ever deepening impact of globalization. In this context, the adaptability of chaplaincy, its ability to 'grow where it is planted' and to flourish in diverse and often unlikely contexts such as the racing industry, suggests that it is likely to become more at a premium than ever before. Although secular Humanists may criticize the public funding of chaplaincy in hospitals, on the whole there is a remarkable amount of good-will towards chaplains by secular organizations and institutions. Chaplains are living Church in the world.

Furthermore, in this changing ecclesial context, the fact that chaplaincy can be a ministry for the whole people of God, lay and ordained, employed and voluntary, part-time and full-time, also makes it particularly apt for a time in which the current level of reliance on full-time ordained clergy is becoming unsustainable. As part of the charism-generated activity of the whole Church (Pickard 2009), it is not surprising that this contextually respon-sive ministry is developing in response to the cultural context of the time.

This book has argued that chaplaincy is in essence dialogic and that this is the source of its strength and vigour. Chaplaincy is not afraid to enter into genuine dialogue, to listen to the experience of others, to be prepared to learn in response to what it hears, and to change in order to remain faithful to its vocation. Part of that commitment to dialogue is the recognition of the need to be in dialogue with those in church-based ministries and with the institutional Church. At the moment, chaplaincy does not have an effective voice within church structures and discourses about mission and ministry. To a significant extent, this is a hidden ministry within the Church, especially in relation to lay and volunteer involvement (Todd, Slater & Dunlop 2014). The purpose of the research on which this book is based was to provide conceptual clarity about the nature of chaplaincy and thus to enable it to be seen and its central significance within the mission of the Church to be recognized. The hope is that when this has been accomplished, genuine dialogue may begin to take place so that there can be mutual enrichment.

Chaplaincy poses fundamental challenges to the institutional Church not only in terms of the Church's current thinking about mission, ecclesiology and ministry but also about what this re-thinking might mean in terms of its *practice*, including the way in which it supports and resources different ministries. Three main areas of need relating to practice require resources: training, support in the development of effective and sustainable chaplaincy roles, and continuing professional development. The meeting of those needs poses an enormous challenge, no different from the challenge of resourcing any other genre of ministry. However, I am hopeful. Chaplaincy is good at finding partnerships and creative ways of working. The point is that if chaplaincy can develop its confidence as a genre of ministry with its own identity and integrity and with a central role to play within the mission of the Church, then it will be better equipped to have a voice within the discourses of the Church. It will no longer be hidden but could be acknowledged as the valuable resource and partner in dialogue that I believe it to be.

What is clear is that chaplains need above all to be able to reflect on their practice in order to gain insight and to develop best practice that can be shared with others. Ways need to be found to enable people to do this through the development of accessible training opportunities, the provision of appropriate supervision and the building up of a community or communities of practice. It is also clear that chaplains need to be encouraged to engage in research and in the evaluation of their work. Keeping basic quantitative data about the work, gaining appropriate feedback from partners and stakeholders, and doing case studies, action research, autoethnography or other kinds of qualitative research, can all help to build up a body of practice-based evidence for the impact and effectiveness of chaplaincy engagement in the public square. It is this evidence that could speak not only to the institutional Church but also to secular organizations which, understandably, want to know what value a chaplaincy service brings to their context.

This is a large agenda which has yet to be developed. I hope that what I have written has brought some clarity to what is being talked about when we talk about chaplaincy today and what its fresh significance might be within the mission of the contemporary Church. The intention is that it will inspire others to talk about chaplaincy and to continue the dialogue and debate. I also hope that those who continue the dialogue will do so in the confidence that this is 'fine work' with its own identity and integrity and that it is central to the missional vocation of the Church, the community of those who are called to gather around the risen Jesus and who are then sent into the world. This book inevitably ends with questions that present challenges to the institutional Church, to those engaged in parish-based ministry and to those engaged in chaplaincy ministry:

- Will the churches have the courage to listen to what the Holy Spirit might be saying through the development of chaplaincy ministry?
- Will chaplains take the opportunity presented by the current interest and growth in chaplaincy ministry to find ways to reflect on practice, engage in research and develop their identity and their voice?
- Will people both in chaplaincy and in church-based ministry be willing to enter into genuine dialogue in order to develop mutual understanding and enrichment?
- Despite the structures and systems that work against it, will the Church seek ways to resource and support a ministry that undoubtedly serves God's mission in the twenty-first century as it has done in centuries past?

It seems as though we have travelled a long way from the certainty of the central ecclesial location of the twelfth-century image of the chaplain in the sanctuary of the Church of St Clemente in Rome. By comparison, the ecclesial location and ministerial identity of the contemporary chaplain may seem ambivalent. However, things are not always as they seem. This book has argued that contemporary chaplaincy ministry does have its own identity and integrity within the Church's ecology of mission and ministry, and that what can be said with certainty is that chaplaincy is of central significance within the mission of the contemporary Church. It holds this significance, because it is able to respond effectively at this particular time to God's call to go out into the world to serve the needs of those whom God loves, and in so doing to embody God's love in and for the whole Creation: '. . . I was sick and you visited me, I was in prison and you came to me' (Matthew 25.36).

Bibliography

Archbishops' Council, 2000, *Common Worship*, London: Church House Publishing.

Archbishops' Council, 2004, *Mission-Shaped Church: Church Planting and Fresh Expressions of Church in a Changing Context*, London: Church House Publishing.

Archbishops' Council, 2014, *From Anecdote to Evidence – Findings from the Church Growth Research Programme 2011–2013*, http://www.churchgrowthresearch.org.uk.

Ballard, P., 2009, 'Locating Chaplaincy: A Theological Note', *Crucible: The Christian Journal of Social Ethics*, July–September, pp. 18–24.

Bayes, P. & Jordan, R., 2010, *A Mixed Economy for Mission: The Journey so Far*, London: The Church of England.

Boff, L., 1977, *Ecclesiogenesis*, London: Collins.

Bosch, D., 1992, *Transforming Mission: Paradigm Shifts in the Theology of Mission*, New York: Orbis.

Bowers, F., 2005, *Report of the Task Group on the Theology of Sector Ministry*, London: Baptist Union of Great Britain.

Braun, F. & Clarke, C., 2006, 'Using Thematic Analysis in Psychology', *Qualitative Research in Psychology* 3, pp. 77–101.

Brown, C., 2009 (2nd edn), *The Death of Christian Britain*, London: Routledge.

Brown, M., 2011, 'Chaplains and the Mission of the Church', *Crucible: The Christian Journal of Social Ethics*, October–December, pp. 3–6.

Buber, M., 1958, *I and Thou*, translated from German by R. Gregor Smith (2nd edn), Edinburgh: T & T Clark.

Cameron, H., 2010, *Resourcing Mission: Practical Theology for Changing Churches*, London: SCM.

Cameron, H., Bahti, D. & Duce, C., 2010, *Talking About God in Practice: Theological Action Research and Practical Theology*, London: SCM.

Cameron, H., Reader, J., Slater, V. & Rowland, C., 2012, *Theological Reflection for Human Flourishing: Pastoral Practice and Public Theology*, London: SCM.

Carrette, J. & King, R., 2005, *Selling Spirituality: The Silent Takeover of Religion*, London & New York: Routledge.

Carroll, M. & Tholstrup, M. (eds), 2001, *Integrative Approaches to Supervision*, London & Philadelphia: Jessica Kingsley.

Churches Working Group, 2008, *How Shall We Sing the Lord's Song in a Strange Land?*, unpublished report.

Cobb, M., 2004, 'The Location and Identity of Chaplains: A Contextual Model', *Scottish Journal of Healthcare Chaplaincy* 7, pp. 10–15.

Cresswell, J., 2007, *Qualitative Inquiry and Research Design*, London: Sage.

Culver, J., 2009, *Chaplaincy Feasibility Study*, London: The Methodist Church of Great Britain.

Davie, G., 1994, *Religion in Britain Since 1945: Believing Without Belonging*, Oxford: Blackwell.

Davison, A. & Milbank, A., 2010, *For the Parish: A Critique of Fresh Expressions*, London: SCM.

Denzin, N. & Lincoln, Y. (eds), 2000, *Handbook of Qualitative Research*, Thousand Oaks, CA: Sage.

Donovan, V., 1978, *Christianity Rediscovered: An Epistle from the Masai*, London: SCM.

Etherington, K., 2007, 'Ethical Research in Reflexive Relationships', *Qualitative Inquiry* 13, pp. 599–615.

Goodhew, D., Roberts, A. & Volland, M., 2012, *Fresh! An Introduction to Fresh Expressions of Church and Pioneer Ministry*, London: SCM.

Handzo, G., Cobb, M., Holmes, C. & Sinclair, S., 2014, 'Outcomes for Professional Health Care Chaplaincy: An International Call to Action', *Journal of Health Care Chaplaincy* 20:2, pp. 43–53.

Hawkins, P. & Shohet, R., 2000, *Supervision in the Helping Professions* (2nd edn), Milton Keynes: Open University Press.

Hayler, P., 2011, 'Doing a New Thing: Chaplaincy as Entrepreneurship', *Crucible: The Christian Journal of Social Ethics,* October–December, pp. 17–24.

Heelas, P., 2002, 'The Spiritual Revolution: From "Religion" to "Spirituality"', in Woodhead, L., Fletcher, P., Kawanami, H. & Smith, D. (eds), *Religion in the Modern World: Traditions and Transformations*, London: Routledge.

Heelas, P. & Woodhead, L., 2005, *The Spiritual Revolution: Why Religion is Giving Way to Spirituality*, Oxford: Blackwell.

Heywood, D., 2011, *Reimagining Ministry*, London: SCM.

Hull, J., 2006, *Mission-Shaped Church: A Theological Response*, London: SCM.

Jones, R., 2010, *Characteristics of Chaplaincy – A Methodist Understanding*, http://www.opensourcechaplaincy.org.uk.

Kolb, D., 1983, *Experiential Learning: Experience as the Source of Learning and Development*, New Jersey: FT Prentice Hall.

Leach, J. & Paterson, M., 2010, *Pastoral Supervision: A Handbook*, London: SCM.

Legood, G., 1999, *Chaplaincy: The Church's Sector Ministries*, London: Cassell.

Lesniak, V., 2005, 'Contemporary Spirituality', in Sheldrake, P. (ed.), *The New SCM Dictionary of Christian Spirituality*, London: SCM.

Methodist Church, 2012, *Chaplaincy Everywhere*, www.opensourcechaplaincy.org.uk/chaplaincy-everywhere/.

Morisy, A., 2004, *Journeying Out: A New Approach to Christian Mission*, London: Continuum.

Morisy, A., 2009, *Bothered and Bewildered: Enacting Hope in Troubled Times*, London & New York: Continuum.

Muir, K. (ed.), 1972, *King Lear*, The Arden Shakespeare, London: Methuen.

Percy, M., 2005, *Engaging with Contemporary Culture: Christian Theology and the Concrete Church*, Aldershot & Burlington: Ashgate.

Percy, M., 2006, *Clergy: Origin of Species*, London: Continuum.

Percy, M., 2008, 'Old Tricks for New Dogs: A Critique of Fresh Expressions', in Nelstrop, L. & Percy, M. (eds), *Evaluating Fresh Expressions: Explorations in Emerging Church*, Norwich: Canterbury Press.

Pickard, S., 2009, *Theological Foundations for Collaborative Ministry*, Farnham: Ashgate.

Rose, J. & Paterson, M. (eds), 2014, *Enriching Ministry: Pastoral Supervision in Practice*, London: SCM.

Rowson, J., 2014, *Spiritualise: Revitalising Spirituality to Address 21st Century Challenges*, London: RSA.

Ryan, B., 2015, *A Very Modern Ministry: Chaplaincy in the UK*, London: Theos.

Shohet, R., 2011, *Supervision as Transformation: A Passion for Learning*, London: Jessica Kingsley.

Simons, H., 2009, *Case Study Research in Practice*, London: Sage.

Slater, V., 2009, 'Chaplaincy in the Community', Oxford Centre for Ecclesiology & Practical Theology, unpublished report.

Slater, V., 2011, 'An Exploration of the Potential Significance for the Mission and Ministry of the Church in England of the Recent Growth in Forms of Chaplaincy in Community Contexts', Cambridge: Anglia Ruskin University, unpublished doctoral paper.

Slater, V., 2013, 'The Fresh Significance of Chaplaincy for the Mission and Ministry of the Church in England: Three Case Studies in Community Contexts', Cambridge: Anglia Ruskin University, unpublished thesis.

Slater, V., 2015, 'Developing Practice Based Evidence', in Swift, C., Cobb, M. & Todd, A. (eds), 2015, *A Handbook of Chaplaincy Studies: Understanding Spiritual Care in Public Places*, Farnham & Burlington: Ashgate.

Spencer, S., 2007, *SCM Study Guide to Christian Mission*, London: SCM.

Stake, R., 1995, *The Art of Case Study Research*, Thousand Oaks, CA: Sage.

Stake, R., 2008, 'Qualitative Case Studies', in Denzin, N. & Lincoln, Y. (eds), *Strategies of Qualitative Inquiry* (3rd edn), Thousand Oaks, CA: Sage.

Steddon, P., 2010, 'Street Church: Fresh Expressions . . . and Beyond?', Oxford, unpublished report.

Swift, C., 2014, *Hospital Chaplaincy in the Twenty-First Century* (2nd edn), Farnham: Ashgate.

Swift, C., Cobb, M. & Todd, A. (eds), 2015, *A Handbook of Chaplaincy Studies: Understanding Spiritual Care in Public Places*, Farnham & Burlington: Ashgate.

Swinton, J., 2001, *Spirituality and Mental Health Care: Rediscovering a Forgotten Dimension*, London: Jessica Kingsley.

Swinton, J., 2002, 'Editorial', *Contact* 138, pp. 1–2.

Swinton, J. & Mowat, H., 2006, *Practical Theology and Qualitative Research*, London: SCM.

Swinton, J. & Pattison, S., 2010, 'Moving Beyond Clarity: Towards a Thin, Vague, and Useful Understanding of Spirituality in Nursing Care', *Nursing Philosophy* 11, pp. 226–37.

Tacey, D., 2004, *The Spirituality Revolution*, London: Routledge.

Tacey, D., 2012, 'Contemporary Spirituality', in Cobb, M., Puchalski, C. & Rumbold, B. (eds), *Oxford Textbook of Spirituality in Healthcare*, Oxford: Oxford University Press.

Tacey, D., 2014, 'Ordinarily Sacred World', *Meditatio Newsletter*, September, pp. 7–8.

Taylor, J., 1984, *The Go-Between God: The Holy Spirit and the Christian Mission*, London: SCM.

Taylor, C., 2007, *A Secular Age*, Cambridge, MA: Belknap Press.

Thomas, G., 2011, *How to Do Your Case Study: A Guide for Students and Researchers*, London: Sage.

Thompson, J., Pattison, S. & Thompson, R., 2008, *SCM Study Guide to Theological Reflection*, London: SCM.

Threlfall-Holmes, M. & Newitt, M. (eds), 2011a, *Being a Chaplain*, London: SPCK.

Threlfall-Holmes, M. & Newitt, M. (eds), 2011b, 'Chaplaincy and the Parish', *Crucible: The Christian Journal of Social Ethics*, October–December, pp. 33–40.

Todd, A., 2007, 'Engaging with Trends in Chaplaincy: Living Faith in Other People's Houses', *Royal Army Chaplaincy Department Journal* 46, pp. 6–9.

Todd, A., 2011, 'Chaplaincy Leading Church in(to) the Public Square', *Crucible: The Christian Journal of Social Ethics*, October–December, pp. 7–15.

Todd, A., Slater, V. & Dunlop, S., 2014, *The Church of England's Involvement in Chaplaincy*, The Cardiff Centre for Chaplaincy Studies & The Oxford Centre for Ecclesiology and Practical Theology.

Volf, M., 1994, *Soft Difference: Theological Reflections on the Relation between Church and Culture in 1 Peter*, www.yale.edu/faith/resources/x_volf_difference.html.

Woodward, J. & Pattison, S. (eds), 2000, *The Blackwell Reader in Pastoral and Practical Theology*, Oxford: Blackwell.

Yin, R. K., 2009, *Case Study Research: Design and Methods* (4th edn), Thousand Oaks, CA: Sage.

Index